Too Young to Be Old is an extremely accessible and conversational book, firmly grounded in relevant research. Dispelling the stereotype of aging as a time of narrowing options, Schlossberg helps readers view retirement and beyond as sets of choices and possibilities.

—**Susan Fuhrman, PhD,** President, Teachers College, Columbia University, New York, NY

Schlossberg has sautéed the psychology of aging into a delicious mixture of insights, advice, and case studies to help those who are coping with the challenges of aging. Drawing on her understanding of transitions, positive psychology, and the key roles that each individual's perceptions play in preparing for and responding to late-life changes, she gives us tools for increasing well-being across the lifespan.

—**Michael A. Smyer, PhD,** Professor of Psychology, Bucknell University, Lewisburg, PA, and founder of *Graying Green: Climate Action for an Aging World*

Age denial and ageism are the great psychological challenge of our time. Prevention and cure come through active hope that is realistic yet positive. This book gives us that hope.

—**Harry R. Moody, PhD,** Retired Vice President (Academic Affairs), AARP

In this upbeat guide, Schlossberg teaches readers how to embrace, understand, and negotiate the transitions of aging. I highly recommend it to all older adults looking to improve their lives.

—**Ken Dychtwald, PhD,** founder and CEO of Age Wave; author of *A New Purpose: Redefining Money, Family, Work, Retirement, and Success*

TOO *Young* TO BE *Old*

LOVE, LEARN, WORK, AND PLAY AS YOU AGE

NANCY K. SCHLOSSBERG, EdD

American Psychological Association • Washington, DC

Published by
APA LifeTools
750 First Street, NE
Washington, DC 20002
www.apa.org

To order
APA Order Department
P.O. Box 92984
Washington, DC 20090-2984
Tel: (800) 374-2721; Direct: (202) 336-5510
Fax: (202) 336-5502; TDD/TTY: (202) 336-6123
Online: www.apa.org/pubs/books
E-mail: order@apa.org

In the U.K., Europe, Africa, and the Middle East, copies may be ordered from
American Psychological Association
3 Henrietta Street
Covent Garden, London
WC2E 8LU England

Typeset in Goudy and Minion by Circle Graphics, Inc., Columbia, MD

Printer: Edwards Brothers, Inc., Ann Arbor, MI
Cover Designer: Naylor Design, Washington, DC

The opinions and statements published are the responsibility of the authors, and
such opinions and statements do not necessarily represent the policies of the
American Psychological Association.

Library of Congress Cataloging-in-Publication Data
Names: Schlossberg, Nancy K., 1929- author.
Title: Too young to be old : love, learn, work, and play as you age / Nancy
    K. Schlossberg, EdD.
Description: First edition. | Washington, DC : American Psychological
    Association, [2017] | Series: LifeTools | Includes bibliographical
    references and index.
Identifiers: LCCN 2016054815| ISBN 9781433827495 | ISBN 1433827492
Subjects: LCSH: Older people—Life skills guides.
Classification: LCC HQ1061 .S336 2017 | DDC 646.7/9—dc23 LC record available at
    https://lccn.loc.gov/2016054815

British Library Cataloguing-in-Publication Data
A CIP record is available from the British Library.

Printed in the United States of America
First Edition

http://dx.doi.org/10.1037/0000031-000

To my three grand girl children—Robin, age 13, Jenny, age 11, and Stevie, age 6. I hope this book will encourage them to view aging as a positive part of life during which they can continue to work, love, and play; and to their parents, Karen Schlossberg and Larry Blair, and Mark and Michele Schlossberg, who laid the groundwork for their development all through life.

Contents

Acknowledgments

Like any project, the writing of a book does not belong to the author alone. In my case, many individuals supported the creation of this book, including the men and women who shared the very personal meaning of their transitions through interviews; the conversation groups held at the Potter YMCA, the Senior Friendship Centers, and the Robert L. Taylor Community Complex; Linda McCarter and Julia Frank-McNeil of the American Psychological Association, who saw the value of publishing a book about adult and aging transitions; and Andrew Gifford of the American Psychological Association, who readied the book for publication. Special thanks go to Paula Falk of the Senior Friendship Centers, who arranged several conversation groups and Erin McLeod of the Senior Friendship Centers, who was there for me in so many ways. I also owe a debt to the intern from New College, Eugenia Quintanilla, who took notes during the conversation groups and often asked relevant questions that kept the conversation moving. Thanks also to

Kathy Black for her support and for connecting me to one of her graduate students, Barbara Bailey, who tackled the references and put them in the proper order and format. Many friends were available to discuss various aspects of the manuscript: Willa Bernhard, Gail and Richard Levin, Kathleen Gurney, Dick Pelton, Roxanne Joffee, Sue Smock, Martin Tolchin, and Paul Weiss. There would be no book without my computer guru, Daniel Gormley, Jr., who saved the manuscript many times when chapters would get lost in cyberspace. Many thanks to Ellen Hoffman, herself an author and a professional editor, who forced me to clarify my thinking, helped shape my material into a book, added value by illuminating "The Money Angle," and suggested the title of this book.

Last but not least, I'd like to thank my partner, Ron Grossman, who supported my long hours at the computer with understanding and who lives life as someone too young to be old with humor, vigor, and consideration.

Introduction

Aging brings many challenges. Sometimes they can seem overwhelming. How do we feel as we confront these challenges? Do we experience love, envy, jealousy, or loneliness? Do we experience a fear of illness and death or a fear of outliving our money and being unable to live on our current income? Or are we excited about the future? Are we excited about finding new interests, new companions, and new surroundings, even as some of the old, comfortable ones fall into the past?

Too Young to Be Old tells a story about transitions and how to handle them, a story about aging and its possibilities, a story about living longer and living well. My mission in this book is to teach the principles of transition theory and positive aging through reporting on the research and sharing real-life experiences, mine and others', so that you can apply these principles to help navigate any major event—or nonevent—in your life.

POSITIVE AGING

Average life expectancy is continuing to trend upward. Nearly 80 million Americans are over the age of 55. Our country has more old people than ever, and they will, on average, be living longer than their forebears. For this ever-growing group, a key question is how to overcome the negative challenges of aging to get the most out of these extra, final years.

Like other phases of our lives, getting old presents us with transitions. Some transitions, such as the death of a spouse, may be forced on us. Others, such as moving from a house to an apartment or relocating to be closer to grandchildren, may be our choice. In this respect, aging is no different from any other phase of life.

It is all too easy to focus on the negatives of aging—illness, physical and mental disability, loss of loved ones—but because our definitions of aging have changed statistically and the average American now looks forward to more healthy years than his or her parents enjoyed, we are seeing an increasing shift in how people think about aging. From a deficit approach that focused on what we lost as we aged, we are shifting to a positive model that acknowledges that older people can make positive contributions to society, and that with aging—surprise!—comes happiness. I, and others who have spent much of our lives studying adult development, call this new model *positive aging*.

The aging process has emerged as a defining and challenging part of my personal life. I find it difficult to think of myself as old-old, but demographically that is who I am. The combination of my personal and professional experience in concert with interviewing many individuals has led me to identify strategies that can boost your happiness and lead to positive aging, no matter what. This book describes these strategies in detail in each of the 11 chapters focusing on these topics:

- talking back to your mirror,
- saying no to ageism,
- embracing change,
- diversifying your coping skills,
- creating your retirement fantasy,
- choosing your place,
- coping with health challenges,
- understanding your family transitions,
- keeping your dance card full,
- going for romance and/or intimacy (if you want it), and
- creating your own path to positive aging.

AGING AND HAPPINESS

Over and over again, we encounter individuals with stories that support the thesis that we can be old and happy at the same time. All around us are examples suggesting that attitude and well-being are linked. Consider the case of an 80-year-old man who is legally blind. He told me he took two subways and a train to travel from Washington, DC, to Baltimore to visit his granddaughter in the hospital. I commented on his ability to do what would seem impossible for most of us. He said, "I made up my mind not to be a tragic figure; I made up my mind to function as independently as I possibly could."

Then there is the case of a 75-year-old woman who has endured many tragedies, including the death of one of her four children from a brain tumor, the death of her husband of 60 years, and the murder of her brother. She is starting a new chapter of her life. Her children helped her get online, where she met a new boyfriend. Now she is focusing on the future.

One of the most memorable anecdotes about positive aging involves a 90-year-old widow who happily displayed the ring she received to signify her engagement to a 95-year-old man. She calls him her fiancé, rather than her boyfriend or companion. They do not plan to marry, but they wanted a symbol of their commitment to each other.

It may seem counterintuitive, but a growing body of research suggests that as people age, they become happier. Various studies tell us that even if we are confronted with difficult challenges, aging does not have to be only a time of worry, fear, and loss. One recent study, reported in *Scientific American Mind*, suggested that we can all look forward to aging happier. This study of several thousand Americans born between 1885 and 1980 revealed "after controlling for variables such as health, wealth, gender, ethnicity, and education, that well-being increases over everyone's lifetime."[1] The exceptions might be people who lived through difficult historical periods, like the Great Depression, or veterans who served in war. Life experience may make a difference in long-term happiness, but people's attitude also may differ depending on which day you ask the question. I often ask people if they are happier as they get older and, as one woman answered, "It depends on when you ask me."

Another researcher studied the paths of individuals from late adolescence to old age. George E. Vaillant, who directed the Harvard Study of Adult Development and wrote a book about it, concluded that successful, positive aging depends on attitude and outlook. For example, Vaillant observed that President Franklin D. Roosevelt "suffered illnesses that would have merited a 100% disability from the Veterans Administration. Clearly, [attitude and] subjective health are as important to aging as objective physical health." He wrote that "whether we live to a vigorous old age lies not so much in our stars or our genes as in ourselves."[2]

It may be tempting to dismiss this example because President Roosevelt was an exceptional person with significant resources. But there is plenty of other validation for this premise. Disabled persons who maintained positive beliefs are more likely to make a recovery, according to a study by Yale epidemiology and psychology professor Becca Levy.[3]

In fact, happiness is now a legitimate avenue for academic study. Martin Seligman, the founder of the positive psychology movement, suggested that we all have an emotional happiness baseline to which we inevitably return. According to Sonja Lyubomirsky, author of *The How of Happiness*, one's happiness level is determined by three things: 50% of happiness comes from one's emotional baseline, 10% from one's life circumstances, and 40% from "intentional activity." This book is about the 40% we can control as we age.[4]

Along with documenting the happiness experienced by older persons, researchers are increasingly examining what it takes to live longer. A 2014 article by the Harvard Medical School, "Living to 100: What's the Secret?", concluded that "if you bring to your life appreciation and respect, and embrace aging with good humor, grace, vigor, and flexibility, you will—at the very least—be happy to grow old."[5] The subtitle of a 2013 report by the Harvard Medical School says it all: *Positive Psychology: Harnessing the Power of Happiness, Mindfulness, and Inner Strength*. The report concluded that "a sunny outlook might protect the heart and brain."[6]

For older persons, as well as for younger ones, attitude can make all the difference between enhancing and enjoying your later years and focusing only on your problems. The people described earlier in this chapter—the newly-engaged 90-year-old woman and the blind 80-year-old who crisscrosses Washington, DC, and Maryland—are survivors who made up their minds to flourish. They do not know it, but they are part of the positive aging movement, which fosters resilience while focusing on one's strengths and happiness. Hundreds of books, articles, and conferences on the topic reflect the degree to which the movement has traction.

So how can we do it? We cannot control our lives to avoid the downs. What we can control is the way we deal with the ups and downs of life; in other words, the resilience with which we manage change, and the strategies we have in place to cope. And we can pay attention to the guidelines and strategies offered in this book, which will help promote positive aging.

ABOUT ME

I am an 87-year-old woman who endured several years as a widow-in-waiting. I have experienced retirement, the loss of my spouse, grief, recovery from grief and from my own physical problems, a return to dating in my 80s, finding a new love, and moving to a retirement community. I lived to tell the tale: As a retired professor of counseling psychology specializing in transitions, I am writing this book informed by my personal experience and by the knowledge and perspective afforded me by some 50 years of study and research, including hundreds of interviews, on the transitions of aging.

I bring two strains of experience to the task—professional and personal. First, I have been a student of adult development and aging since I was an assistant professor at Wayne State University and taught my first course in adult development at age 35. My subsequent career as a professor at the University of Maryland consisted of university teaching, conducting research, and writing nine books about adult transitions. Over my long career I have had the opportunity to interview hundreds of individuals and hear their stories about their personal lives and transitions. Even since my official retirement from academia at age 67, my professional life has continued to be personally rewarding, with extensive opportunities for speaking and writing.

When I started teaching more than 50 years ago, aging was an abstract concept to me. Now, at 87, aging is no longer an abstraction. My own experience echoes that of the author Betty Friedan, who described her evolution while writing *The Fountain of Age*: "When I started this book," Friedan said, "it was about them. Now it's about me."[7] When I started studying and teaching about aging, it was about them. Now it is very much about me. So I bring my personal and professional lenses to the topic of how we can be positive agers.

In addition, I have experienced a new kind of transition—less observable, but as potent. For the first time, I felt the clock ticking and realized there are nonnegotiable limits. Always before, if I did not reach a particular goal I could say to myself, "There is time to regroup and try it a different way." Now I feel differently. The transition of thinking of myself as having limited options has been gradual. But at the same time, it is an exciting period. I am curious about the future. How will I deal with this final period of my life? I am determined to think positively, although that is not always easy. It is different. I say my age without trying to hide it.

After reading one of my published articles on aging, a woman I did not know called me up to say, "I wish you were my next-door neighbor so I could talk to you about my challenges and issues." The purpose of this book is to communicate what I have learned as a retired professor of counseling psychology, as an author of nine books on transitions, and as someone who is actually living life as an old person. This book is for that woman who took the trouble to call me up, as well as for anyone else who is looking for guidance on how to successfully navigate the uncharted territory of getting old.

THE PLAN OF THIS BOOK

Too Young to Be Old is divided into four sections. Each of the 11 chapters recommends a broad strategy to help readers through the many transitions that typically occur during life's later years.

Part I, Resolve Your Love–Hate Relationship With Aging, takes a frank look at the feelings that we experience as we age. It pinpoints our feeling that, even though we get the AARP membership offer, the wrinkles, the gray hair, and the Medicare card, we still feel young inside, and it suggests that some of our frustrations may emerge from our own ageism. Chapter 1, "Talk Back to Your Mirror," suggests ways to overcome what is often the shock and dismay of how aging has changed us physically. Chapter 2, "Just Say No to Ageism," confronts an issue that is often subtle and unrecognized, yet one that plays an important role in our sense of self and our possibilities as we age.

Part II, Understand Transitions, provides the context for understanding the structure of any transition. Chapter 3, "Embrace Change," outlines the model of transitions I developed after 35 years of studying transitions. I describe the role of timing in transitions—is the transition on time, off time, out of time, or no time/nonevent? Chapter 4, "Diversify Your Coping Skills," explains basic coping strategies that can help you master the many transitions connected with aging.

Part III, Navigate the Many Transitions of Aging, shows how the transition framework plays out in four transitions commonly experienced as we age. Each of the four chapters dissects one of these challenges—retiring (Chapter 5, "Create Your Own Retirement Fantasy"), deciding where to live (Chapter 6, "Choose Your Place: Location, Location, Location"), coping with health issues (Chapter 7, "Cope With Health Challenges"), and coping with family issues (Chapter 8, "Understand Your Family Transitions")—and suggests how you can ace those transitions.

Part IV, Create the New You, focuses on how you can approach the future positively. Chapter 9, "Keep Your Dance Card Full: Pay Attention to Friends, Family, and Fun," underscores the importance of social engagement, and Chapter 10, "Go for Romance (If You Want It)," suggests that if you are still interested in romance, you should be open to it, regardless of your age. The final chapter, "Create Your Own Happiness:

Your Path to Positive Aging," describes ways that you can create your own happiness as you explore and improvise your road to positive aging.

THE RESEARCH FOR THIS BOOK

I specifically targeted several groups and individuals to learn more about the transitions discussed throughout the book. I participated in what I called "conversation groups" around the topic of health, money, and caregiving. I met with people at a senior center, a YMCA, a community center in a low-income area, and a healing circle at a library in a low-income area. In addition, I conducted 25 interviews with selected individuals.

SUMMARY

Aging will continue to challenge us. Mastering these challenges is the goal of this book. Whether we are 60, 70, 80, 90, or even 100, we need all the signposts we can find to help us face the challenges ahead. This book is about the drama of our futures, which will be filled with unexpected twists and turns. We will be forced to improvise as we deal with the unknown. This is a book about how to learn, work, love, and play all through life.

I

RESOLVE YOUR LOVE–HATE RELATIONSHIP WITH AGING

1

Talk Back to Your Mirror

We face a conundrum: People desperately want to live longer, and yet, at the same time, they go to great lengths not to look like they are living longer. Over and over, we hear ourselves saying, "I can't believe what I see in the mirror." In the article "Last Word: The French Do It Better," one woman was quoted as saying the following:

> Nowadays it is a shock to catch sight of myself in a mirror. I think, "This can't be true. Someone has waved a hand and turned me into a woman of 80." . . . When I meet my friends, I am invariably shocked. What wicked fairy has changed . . . (them) into aging females?[1]

To change their image, women, and now men, are flocking to plastic surgeons. According to the American Society of Plastic Surgeons, both women and men age 55 and older have undergone procedures like face-lifts, eyelid operations, and breast lifts or reductions.[2]

Complementing—or perhaps staving off—the cosmetic surgery for aging Americans is the annual purchase of more than $2 billion in antiaging skin products; anti-aging cream sells well even during hard economic times. A marketing survey suggests that fighting back against our aging appearance will prompt an increase in the global expenditure for antiaging products and services from the $249 billion spent on these products in 2012 to $346 billion in 2018.[3] One woman in her early 70s informed one of my conversation groups that "dyeing your hair is essential. You can look like someone's sister or aunt but not the mother."

What does this mean? This preoccupation reflects our love/hate relationship with aging, our fear of aging, and our resistance to its reality. Furthermore, the demographic reality is that nearly one in five Americans will be over the age of 65 by 2030.[4]

WHAT DO WE FEAR?

Aging is scary. One woman told me,

> I feel very schizophrenic about aging. I would say I never felt better in life; I did not know life could feel like this. Yet it does not look like a very positive future! It is a lot of endings . . . there is a real letting go of just about everything.

Another woman said, "I think of old people having bad breath, stooped over, with hair growing randomly out of their faces." When one 8-year-old child told her grandmother that she was getting old, her grandmother asked, "How do you know?" "The bumps on your hands," answered the granddaughter.

We fear that our looks will give us away. We fear that we will become invisible and marginalized. Many women complain that no one whistles at them when they walk by anymore. We fear that we will outlive our money; that we will have a horrible end-of-life illness; that we will have less fun, less money, less sex, fewer opportunities. We fear that we will get Alzheimer's disease.

According to Ted C. Fishman, author of *Shock of Gray*, we live with many realities of aging. In a speech, he presented two very different realities of aging presented by his family. His father was ill for 16 years, and Fishman rushed to his father's deathbed repeatedly.[5] On the other hand, his 83-year-old mother, who was in the audience for his speech, was about to take a major trip. We fear that we will be like Fishman's father, not his mother.

The underlying fear is the fear of dying—not the fear of death. I was flying home from Europe once, when the pilot explained that we might be flying into a hurricane. I could feel my heart thumping and thought, "How can I survive an 8-hour plane trip thinking about a hurricane?" Then I asked myself, "What is the worst that can happen?" and the answer was, "I will die." Then I tricked myself and said,

> Let me think about the advantages of dying. First, I have not yet outlived my money, so my adult children would inherit a little money—money that would be helpful to them and their families. Second, I would escape a long horrible, end-of-life illness.

In other words, I faced down the worst scenario I could imagine at that moment.

We spend a great deal of time thinking about aging: Do we look old, do we have more wrinkles, is our new birthday leading us into the scenario that we are old and are "losing it?" I have heard 50-year-olds, 70-year-olds, and 90-year-olds proclaim that they hate the new number. In one of my conversation groups, a woman who was approaching her 70th birthday shared her feelings of fear, particularly her fear of the end and of losing her identity. "I do not feel old but the label *old* is becoming part of my identity." How do you feel about telling your age?

WE CAN AGE WITH PANACHE

Despite the fears and problems, keep in mind that according to the Pew Research Center on Social and Demographic Trends, getting old is not nearly as bad as people think. A survey on aging among a nationally representative sample of 2,969 adults, which looked at aspects of everyday life ranging from mental acuity and physical dexterity to sexual activity and financial security, found a sizable gap between the expectations that young and middle-age adults have about old age and the actual experiences reported by older adults themselves.[6] These disparities come into sharpest focus when survey respondents are asked about negative benchmarks often associated with aging, such as illness, memory loss, an inability to drive, an end to sexual activity, a struggle with loneliness and depression, and difficulty paying bills. In every instance, older adults report experiencing these negative benchmarks at lower levels (often far lower) than younger adults report expecting to encounter them when they grow old.

Many people think older adults are not happy. But the same factors that predict happiness among younger adults—good health, good friends, and financial security—by and large predict happiness among older adults.

An AARP article by Beth Howard, "What to Expect in Your 70s and Beyond," suggested that the 70s are the happiest years of your life. Howard quoted Laura Carstensen, director of the Stanford Center on Longevity, as attributing this impression to experience: "As you get older, you know that bad times are going to pass. . . . You also know that good times will pass, which makes those good times even more precious." In the same article, Bob Knight, professor of gerontology and psychology at the USC Davis School of Gerontology, suggested that another factor that may contribute to a positive life in your 70s is having more control over your emotions, which makes it easier to rule out anger, stress, and negativity.[7]

Howard emphasized that we have the ability to prevent, or at least ameliorate, health issues by taking actions, such as remaining intellectually active to ward off loss of brain function and exercising to maintain muscle strength. Aging does not have to terminate your sex life, according to Howard, quoting studies showing that people in their 70s have active sex lives despite often-encountered erectile dysfunction among men and vaginal dryness among women. This type of research offers hope that we can in fact slow down or even stave off some of the physical effects of aging that we would prefer not to experience. In other words, we can "age with panache"—with flair, verve, and vigor. Ursula, who is about to celebrate her 100th birthday, said that aging with panache means "dressing carefully each day, looking as good as one can; it means smiling and not making people feel sorry for you; it means being involved, staying interesting. It means living life to the fullest."

There are many examples of people aging with panache. At the age of 62, Mikhail Baryshnikov danced at the 2010 Ringling Museum International Festival on an empty stage in front of a screen projecting a video of a young man dancing. The young man was Baryshnikov at an earlier age, and in the video, Baryshnikov was dancing with an even younger version of himself. There were three dancers: the younger, the older, and the shadow. At 62, he could no longer leap in the air, but he still created thrilling performances. He had style!

But you do not have to be famous to age with panache. There are many ways to do it. A woman who lives in a nursing home wears colored flat shoes to match her sweaters. She explained, "Even though I can no longer wear high heels, I don't have to be dowdy." A retired investigative reporter no longer writes several stories a week. He paces himself and writes a bimonthly column. An 87-year-old man, who had been a mover and a shaker, is currently trapped in a home with around-the-clock caregivers for his wife, who has Alzheimer's. He has enough money to do whatever pleases him, but no freedom. He feels guilty leaving his wife, but uncharacteristically, he took a 5-day vacation. There, he met a woman and began a romance. Where this romance will go is uncertain, but he made some important observations. He said people characterize old people, not realizing they have the same emotions and dreams they have always had. What he has missed was romance, fun, excitement—the joy of holding a woman. He and his friend went to a movie and held hands the entire time, just as he had done in his youth.

RESOLVE THE CONUNDRUM

It is too easy to be lulled into a feeling that life is better—that old people are happy, control their negative emotions, and enjoy love and romance. However, we cannot ignore the counterargument—that life is full of disappointment, loss, and sadness, that all around friends are dying or worse, living with miserable health challenges. We do not need to hide our limitations, but we do need to seek new opportunities and new possibilities. That is what aging with panache is all about—figuring out your own lifetime of possibilities. Of course, that is easier said than done.

It is fine to talk back to the mirror and say, "I want to look as good as I can." For some of us, applying anti-aging cream every night or wearing brightly colored clothing serves as a positive, tangible sign to ourselves and others that we can act as young as we feel. But we should not delude ourselves into thinking that physical touch-ups will get us through the emotional changes, disappointments, and frustrations that can result from the loss and illness of friends or family, and from the fear that our "normal" routines are gone forever.

Remember the woman at the beginning of this chapter who said she "could not believe" that she and her friends had turned into "aging females?" She also said something about reconnecting with her friends: "Something magical happens. I call it 'the second look.' The mask of age falls away, and there are my friends as they existed for me always: young, smiling, and the dear persons that I remember."[1] She looked into the mirror, saw her friends as they were on that day, and then mentally reframed the image to imagine and relate to them as they always were.

YOUR TO-DO LIST

It is the balance of love and hate that counts. If your hate about aging outweighs your love for your age, you need to figure out a way to turn the negatives into positives. Here are a few tips:

- **Reframe the negatives:** List the negatives and try to look at each one in a different way.

- **Connect with people:** If you see only losses and feel lonely, figure out some ways to connect with new groups. One woman realized her world was narrowing. She decided to go online as a way to meet new people.
- **Count your blessings:** What is good about your life? What gives you fun and comfort? One woman had many friends and activities but dwelt on what she did not have. She had a choice—focus on what she did not have or on what she did.
- **Try something you did not think you could do:** Try something that will make your friends, your neighbors, and your family say, "Now that's panache!" For example, former President George H. W. Bush defied expectations by doing a tandem parachute jump on his 90th birthday.

So, do not be afraid to look in the mirror. You might be surprised by what you see.

2

Just Say No to Ageism

Koreans celebrate their 60th birthday as a joyous occasion that marks the passage into old age. In India, multigenerational families often live in the same household; younger family members seek advice from the elders on issues such as finances and family conflicts. In Japan, each September the country celebrates Revere the Elderly Day with special programs and gifts for the 80-and-older crowd; citizens who reach 100 receive a silver sake cup as a sign of respect.

These are only some of the cultures in which aging brings respect and admiration. Unfortunately, these cultures stand in contrast to that of the United States, where all too often we disparage people because of their age, reinforcing the stereotype that physical and mental decline is an inevitable sign of decreasing competence and relevance. The words we use for this type of attitude are *ageism* or *age bias*, and we can find it all around us if we look. Dr. Robert Neil Butler, a physician and gerontologist who was the first director of the National

Institute on Aging, coined the term *ageism*. He defined the concept as a combination of three connected elements: prejudicial attitudes toward older people, old age, and the aging process; discriminatory practices against older people; and institutional practices and policies that perpetuate stereotypes about elderly people.[1]

Sometimes ageism is subtle. A woman in one of my conversation groups explained that she deflects age bias "by dyeing my hair [and] not telling my age. Most of my friends in the building where I live are 10 years younger and at work my age never comes up. I am 76 but present myself as 66." She goes to all this trouble because "I still want to be seen as relevant!" In other words, she feels that society would be dismissive of her if people knew her real age. Linda, a member of my water aerobics class, dyed her hair when it turned white after chemotherapy because her grandchildren "begged" her to color it so she would look young again.

Sometimes ageism is not so subtle. Let me make a confession. One night, I arrived at a party at the same time as a convertible. The car's top was down, and two people were sitting in the front and two more were in the back. My first thought was, "How nice to be going to a party with younger people." I was startled when I realized they were all residents of a nearby retirement community. My thought process reflected my bias about aging—if you live in a retirement community you would not be in a convertible, especially in the backseat. I was doing what we all do all the time—categorizing people by age. Despite the fact that I have studied and written professionally about the topic, I too am sometimes guilty of age bias. Even someone society regards as "elderly" or "old" may have stereotypes about other people of similar age.

AGE BIAS IS EVERYWHERE

Why write about age bias in a book about positive aging? Very simply, our attitudes about what is appropriate to do at various ages and what we think middle-age and older people should be doing will influence how we will approach our own transitions. Whenever we think someone is too old to wear sleeveless clothes, too old to still live at home with parents, or too young to run for office, we are categorizing by age. We hear remarks about an 80-year-old woman who married a 68-year-old man or a 90-year-old man marrying a 60-year-old woman and judge their behavior on the basis of what we believe is appropriate.

So how does ageism crop up? It happens often in the language we use, reinforcing the "prejudicial attitudes toward older people." It also crops up when older people are underrepresented in the media. George Gerbner and Nancy Signorielli, both with the Annenberg School of Communications, compared the demographic reality of various groups with their TV representation, concluding that television celebrates youth, as well as certain white-collar professions, whereas it neglects the elderly along with blue-collar workers.[2] The late-night television shows are an especially common source of stereotyping of older people. Nancy

Perry Graham, the editor of *AARP The Magazine*, wrote in the January 2010 issue,

> Scarcely an evening goes by that David Letterman . . . does not mock a certain 73-year-old politician with lines such as "During the presidential campaign, Sarah [Palin] had to cut up John McCain's meat for him." Recently Jimmy Fallon . . . announced that the family of a 70-year-old man who had run his 163rd marathon would celebrate by "taking him out to a five-star emergency room."[3]

Similarly, many birthday cards for people over 50 have negative comments about aging, like, "It is all downhill after 40." These cards and the jokes made on television are merely the tip of the iceberg. We are routinely bombarded with messages that older people have less—less energy, less opportunities, less sex, less money—than those who are younger. Except for wrinkles, it is all about less. This is despite the fact that a Duke University study showed that some 20% of people over age 65 have sex lives that are better than ever before if "you stay interested, stay healthy, stay off medications, and have a good mate."[3]

Another fount of age bias is the job market—an arena that has become increasingly important as more people in their 60s, 70s, and 80s seek employment as a financial necessity in a sluggish economy. An email from an unemployed 60-year-old, who had been CEO of a nonprofit that closed, described the result of a 2-year job search: "It is come to this, for the time being—Uber driving and substitute teaching. Good opportunities on the horizon, but it is been a slog. Age bias is alive and well!"

I interviewed a 62-year-old journalist and asked him if he experienced age bias. His answer was a resounding yes. He reported that with recent budget cuts, he was fearful for his job. "We are afraid that we will be fired so that younger, less expensive reporters can be hired. So, yes, it is always in our minds, and we are constantly having to prove ourselves." A woman from Texas in her 60s searched for work for 5 years after she lost her job at a mortgage company:

> They see gray hair and they just write you off. . . . They are afraid to hire you, because they think you are a health risk. You know, you might make their premiums go up. They think it will cost more money to invest in training you than it is worth because you might retire in 5 years. . . . Not that they say any of this to your face.[4]

The words may not be explicit, but as many others discover, the message is definitely a reality.

EFFECTS OF AGE BIAS

How do these messages manifest themselves in our day-to-day life? Many older people allow the manifestations of ageism to influence their own attitudes and behavior. Many report feeling as if they are invisible and marginalized, reflecting a sense of loss or irrelevance. University of Florida professor and gerontologist Kathy Black, the lead researcher on the project *Aging With Dignity*, found that "ageism was the second most mentioned challenge to dignity, and particularly to self-identity." A 79-year-old man commented to her, "ageism is alive . . . as people see wrinkles, gray hair, or frailties, [they] respond in a dismissive manner."[5] Black found that this experience was common, as a 74-year-old man commented,

> I think we have all experienced it, whether we are conscious of it all of the time or not, is when you get to a certain age bracket, people do look at you as if "it is time for you to be on the shelf," or worse yet, "you are taking up space."

Surrounded by such negative messages, we use various tactics to attempt to disguise our chronological age. One way to do this, as discussed in the previous chapter, is to try to alter our appearance with cosmetic surgery.

Some people will not tell their age. They do not want others to make assumptions about them—about their competency or their behavior. I was the keynote speaker at the 2015 annual meeting of Masterpiece, an organization designed to encourage those living in retirement communities to stay engaged intellectually, spiritually, physically, and socially. The purpose of the meeting was to chart new paths to positive aging. Even though I was about to move into a retirement community myself, I could not admit this at the meeting. I did not lie; I merely avoided saying it, even though it was relevant to that meeting. I was afraid if the group knew I was moving into a retirement community, I would be seen as "over the hill."

This incident made me realize how pervasive and insidious age bias is. If I, who studies the subject, can feel that I must camouflage or downplay my own age, how must others feel? Even more important, what is the impact of age bias on the individual? Age stereotyping limits options. People begin to think, "I am too old to think about. . . ." For some people, they may be too old for romance, others they may be too old to apply for a particular job, and others may be too old to move to a new city. Psychologists Hazel Markus and Paula Nurius study the ways people think of themselves in the future, what they called *possible selves*.[6] They concluded that older people have fewer possible selves than younger people. When people sense that someone judges them negatively because of their age, this can be internalized and limit their future vision and behavior. That could have convinced Betty White not to continue acting and John Glenn not to participate in another space mission.

CHALLENGE AGE BIAS

Whether the attitude emanates from the broader society or whether it emerges from within our own aging personality, the effect is the same: We are discouraged from living life fully, from doing things that may contribute to our happiness, and even from contributing to society as a whole. A number of experts have suggested ways that our society can help change the aging landscape by confronting ageism, not giving in to it.

Disrupt Aging: A Bold New Path to Living Your Best Life at Every Age by Jo Ann Jenkins, CEO of the AARP, is a most dramatic and effective challenge to age bias. She disagrees with the common notion that, for example, 70 is the new 50. No, 70 is the real 70. The AARP press release about the book states, "Ms. Jenkins says *Disrupt Aging* is not about defying aging or denying aging. It is about owning your age."[7]

Change Our Language

One way to do this is to harness the power of language to provide positive models and images. The Harvard University and MetLife study *Reinventing Aging* concluded that "new language, imagery, and stories are needed to help boomers and the general public reenvision the role and value of elders and the meaning and purpose of one's later years." The report proposed that we eliminate words that convey a negative image of aging as being dependent, frail, and "losing it." The report also warned against going to the other extreme and extolling seniors as "eternally young."[8]

The experience of the women's movement offers a useful lesson on language. Years ago, people in general were referred to by the term *he*. Women were referred to as *Mrs.* or *Miss*, identifying them primarily on the basis of their marital status, as opposed to their gender. With concerted efforts by public figures and media organizations, language changes occurred and filtered down into the common parlance. Women came to be represented as part of the collective—as in the terms *men and women* or *people*, instead of the terms *he* or *men*. Now women have the option to identify themselves as *Ms.*, signifying that marital status is not necessarily the primary characteristic of their identity. We need to do the same when talking about aging. We must stop saying things like, "I moved into an old people's home," and call other people on it when they use these types of biased expressions.

Encourage Intergenerational Contact

Another way to take a stand against age bias is to encourage more intergenerational contact. Maddy Dychwald, cofounder of the think tank Age Wave, suggested *reverse mentorships*, opportunities for older people to learn from younger ones, especially about technology. This type of activity can benefit both age groups: Younger people can learn from the experience and accumulated knowledge of the older individuals they are mentoring. *In the Mix*,[9] a PBS series aimed at a teenage audience, profiled projects in which youths were exposed to the experience and wisdom of the older generation. They highlighted the example of a senior day center in New York where intergenerational programs helped the teens realize that "seniors are not boring, and can offer useful advice on life and career choices." To be successful, however, it appears that these efforts need to be carefully designed. "Programs designed around long-term, more sustained contact have resulted in more positive attitudes toward older people" than have those that are short-term, according to researchers who analyzed numerous studies of intergenerational programs structured around shared educational, recreational, and volunteer activities. Success was also more likely when the activities included "quality contact, such as encouraging empathy or sharing personal information."

Proselytize Aging

Dr. Bill Thomas, a graduate of Harvard Medical School, changed the focus of his career from a practicing geriatrician to a musician singing about the joys of aging. Thomas gave up his medical practice in favor of proselytizing. His "The Age of Disruption" tour has been taking him through the United States and Canada on a mission to raise public consciousness—strumming a guitar and presenting a stage show that touts a "post-adulthood" period when age and experience are associated with enrichment rather than decrepitude. "He believes that his generation, which reinvented what it means to be young, should now be reinventing what it means to grow old." In essence, he argues, the goal is "normalizing the entire lifespan instead of separating and stigmatizing one part as something different." Thomas is proud to be called old; he values what he called *postadulthood* and fights the insidiousness of age bias with music and drama.[10]

We cannot all make proselytizing about aging our primary mission in life. But Thomas does set a good example for us. When someone makes a negative or disparaging comment about aging or an older person, try calling them on it politely and suggesting a more positive comment as an alternative.

YOUR TO-DO LIST

As our society ages, we hope that the stigma of being old or appearing old will fade away. But this is unlikely to happen unless we become a part of the change. It behooves all of us as individuals to recognize age bias when we see it or hear it, as well as to try to combat it. Instead of deprecating ourselves because of our age, our wrinkles, or our forgetfulness, we need to challenge ourselves to figure out how to face our own aging with verve and style. We must be part of changing the aging landscape. Here are some things we can do to take positive action toward this goal and some ways you personally might combat age bias in the course of your daily life:

- **Face your own ageism:** Two quizzes can help you do this. One is developed by Project Implicit, a nonprofit organization of researchers interested in uncovering our assumptions about different types of bias (https://implicit.harvard.edu/implicit/). The other quiz, "Facts on Aging," consists of 50 true-or-false questions designed to reveal your attitude about older people's physical and mental health status and their creativity, adaptability, and social roles.[11]

37

- **Vow never to assume that you are too old to do something:** When presented with an opportunity—a hike in the mountains, a chance to teach Sunday School to children at your church, learning a new skill—analyze the opportunity objectively and make a decision on the basis of your mental and physical status and on the timing of the opportunity, not just on your age.
- **Be open to new possibilities:** Martha, a 65-year-old physician living in Boston, assumed she was too old for romance. When she went home to Little Rock to be with her dying mother, she reconnected with her high-school boyfriend. They ended up getting married; she closed down her practice, moved to Little Rock, and is working in public health there. She never expected to marry, never expected to live in Little Rock, and never expected to be so happy. We need to keep in mind that life is full of surprises, many of which are happy ones, regardless of our age.
- **Respond to ageist comments:** Explain why you think the comment is inappropriate, and turn it into a positive statement. If a friend comments, "Women over 50 should not wear a sleeveless dress," you might suggest that rather than an arbitrary age standard, the decision about clothing style should be based on what the individual feels is comfortable.
- **Talk about ageism with your older friends:** Comparing notes on your own experiences or observations can be good way to raise awareness of the issue.

- **Acknowledge that attitudes about age develop from an early time in our life:** Realize that age bias has potentially limiting, negative effects on individuals of all ages. Consider the 5-year-olds who are already computer literate, and how they would lose ground academically if a parent or teacher believed they were too young to learn to use the computer.

II

UNDERSTAND TRANSITIONS

3

Embrace Change

Elizabeth Bernstein, a columnist for *The Wall Street Journal*, described the upheaval when her offices were moved to a new building. Bernstein described how the experience, including the emergence of adolescent feelings and the changes in routines (e.g., where to find the bathroom), affected her relationships and assumptions about the way life would be for her.[1] She had it right. A seemingly innocuous change, like moving to a new office space, can, in fact, make us queasy. I studied transitions for over 35 years and found that any change over which you have no control can have extraordinary consequences. If a small transition, such as changing offices, can have such an impact, imagine what a big transition, such as divorce, death, or relocating a thousand miles away to a new state, can do to you.

When Ruth's husband presented her with the prospect of retiring and moving to Florida from Connecticut, she told me she was paralyzed with fear. I cried until my mascara dripped on my clothing and my children worried that I was having a teeny weeny nervous breakdown. . . . I was crying at the idea of retirement . . . I wondered what I would do all day . . . I had worked on a news-paper . . . not exactly *The New York Times* . . . but it was intoxicating.

Despite her first reaction, Ruth went along with her husband's suggestion to relocate. At first, she felt she was "more in God's waiting room than in paradise," but several years later, still ensconced in Florida, Ruth is content with her life. "I sit on the terrace and watch the pelicans and I enjoy watching my husband enjoy-ing [life]. . . . I have started painting, and my work is regularly shown in art shows. I still write occasional articles for the paper. And I am part of a memoir [writing] group."

So how did Ruth create a positive lifestyle from what she initially viewed as a catastrophe, one that could compromise her identity and her sense of purpose? She strengthened herself by sharing her concerns with her husband, as well as by talking to friends new and old. When she joined the memoir group, she met someone who became a close friend. Her art became a new purpose in her life and smoothed her way into the community as she looked for and found galleries that would show her work. Through these activities, she made many new friends. Ten years after the big move, Ruth's identity and sense of purpose remain intact. As she says—"I did not die in Florida."

DISSECT YOUR TRANSITIONS

We toss around the term *transition* as if it means the same thing to everyone. When I first started studying the topic, it was perplexing. Is a geographical move as big of a transition as retirement? Is each transition unique, or are there commonalities that would help us understand and manage them more effectively? My work over the years, studying at least 15 different transitions in depth, has led me to the conclusion that although each person and each transition is unique, there are commonalities that, if understood, would help us stay in charge.

The goal is to identify the characteristics that will explain why you are coping well with one transition but not another and, furthermore, why several people experiencing the same transition have wildly different experiences. Some people embrace change, but most of the people I have interviewed over the years found change, even happy change, discombobulating. Next, we will see why change, even desired change, is so challenging and how you can take the tiger by the tail.

Transitions are never simple. My job is to dissect them so that you will have the tools for assessing any transition. This builds on the ancient idiom about how you can catch a fish for someone or teach them how to fish. This book is written as a way to teach you how to fish. To start, we need to look at the components of a transition, as it will provide clues to better understand it.

The outcome of a particular set of transitions depends on understanding three key factors:

- *Degrees of change:* To what degree does the transition change your life—your *roles, relationships, routines,* and *assumptions?* The bigger the change, even if it is positive, the more the stress.
- *Timing of your transition:* Is the transition on time, off time, out of time, or no time?
- *The transition process:* Where you are in the transition—the beginning, middle, or resolution. Resolution is achieved when you have embraced new *roles, relationships, routines,* and *assumptions.*

Degrees of Change

Transitions are events (e.g., marriage, divorce, retirement, becoming a grandparent) or nonevents (e.g., not getting a desired promotion, not getting pregnant, not being able to afford retirement) that change your life through your *roles, relationships, routines,* and *assumptions.* But whether you have time to think ahead or not, it is important to be aware that every transition has the potential to alter these four crucial aspects of your life.

To illustrate, consider two common transitions that may appear to have little in common: the birth of a child and retirement. Becoming a new parent adds a new and demanding role with tremendous responsibility. Relationships with your spouse or partner and other family members are transformed. Your daily routine is dominated by the needs of a child, as much or more than by your own needs. Previous assumptions about issues, such as where to live (e.g., the neighborhood with the best schools) or how much money to save (e.g., retirement vs. college), suddenly become obsolete.

The transition to retirement also brings changes in your *roles*, *relationships*, *routines*, and *assumptions*. You lose your identity as a worker. You may or may not continue to have relationships with your coworkers, and if you do, they occur in a different context. If you have a spouse or partner, you may need to adjust to spending many more hours in that person's company. Regardless of your previous schedule, leaving behind the demands of work will inevitably change your routine, possibly affecting everything, from what time you get up and go to sleep to when and where you eat your meals, to how you spend your time. Assumptions about important issues, such as how to survive on your retirement income instead of a salary and even where to live, also will be subject to change.

These two examples highlight the fact that it is not the transition per se that is critical but how much it alters the basic structure of your life. That explains why two people experiencing what seems to be the same transition are, in fact, experiencing different ones. One new grandparent may be enjoying the new role, relishing the change in routines, assumptions, and relationships, whereas another, who is forced to take over child care duties, may be experiencing a more intense change. One may be experiencing joy; the other, almost certainly, may have mixed emotions.

Timing of Your Transitions

Throughout our lives, we experience transitions. From a time perspective, they fall into four categories. Sociologist Gunhild Hagestad called the transitions that emerge at the time we expect them *on-time transitions*. The ones that occur when we would not normally expect them, are referred to as *off-time transitions*. Changes that seem to isolate you from your own routine are *out-of-time transitions*.[2] Finally, there is the transition you expect, wait for, and plan for but that simply does not happen. I call these *no-time transitions* or *nonevents*. The following examples illustrate these types of transitions and their potential impact on how you live your life.

Analyzing the timing can provide a clue for understanding your reaction to your transition. We hear that 50 is the new 40, and then that 65 is the new 50. Women in their 40s have babies; 25-year-olds live in their parents' homes. Some people are still working at age 85, 20 years past the "official retirement age."

For Americans 50 and older, many of the preconceptions we have held about what to do at what age are being challenged by what is going on around us.

Society holds assumptions about the "right" time in life to do certain things, whether it is moving out of your parents' home, getting married, or retiring. As we age, however, we may become more and more conscious that the world around us does not seem to be operating on these same assumptions. When our own life pattern does not follow these assumptions, it can be hard to adjust.

For example, a 90-year-old man sat crying because his 27-year-old grandson was diagnosed with cancer. The grandfather was devastated not only for his grandson but also for his daughter, who was supporting his grandson. This brought back memories of his other daughter, who had died of cancer at the age of 31. These deaths were off-time transitions. As he said, "I wish I could trade places with my grandson."

On-Time Transitions

Imagine that your daughter finishes college and gets the job of her dreams. After many decades, your marriage continues to be strong. You and your spouse are healthy, and anticipating an interesting but relaxing retirement. One woman toasted her husband of 61 years by saying, "Living together is a sweet, wonderful period of our lives." Usually, when we are on time we feel our life is following the script—we are okay, happy even.

But there can be exceptions and sometimes on-time transitions are unhappy. For example, Jeanne was of an age considered on time for a move from independent living to a nursing home, but she still viewed the transition as negative. To help her get through it, she gathered a support team—her son, her granddaughter, her best friend, her doctor, her former law partner and his wife, a financial adviser, and an interior decorator. With their help, she was able to make good judgments about where to live and how to pay for it. The interior decorator helped convert the tiny, sterile room into an attractive one, complete with purple bedspread, purple walls, and purple bathroom features, which complemented Jeanne's own paintings. It took a village to help Jeanne with the move, but it was worth it because the result was a comfortable, attractive setting about which she could feel good.

Off-Time Transitions

All of us have internal clocks that suggest what it is appropriate to do at each age. The psychologist Bernice Neugarten labeled this your *social clock*.[3] We have all heard people say things like, "I am too old to still live at home," "I am too old to go back to school," "I am too old to get divorced," and "My biological clock is ticking." Each culture has a different timetable for life events—when to go to school, when to have children, when to marry, and when to retire. These timetables influence our reactions to our circumstances. When your life, or the lives of others who are close to you, does not proceed according to the generally accepted timetable, this can cause unhappiness or even feelings of failure.

Gail reminisced sadly about the untimely death of her father, "My father died 6 months before he would have received his pension from the Navy." Aside from the sorrow about his death, Gail was upset by the fact that it was off time. In another example, Sue had hoped for a particular job; however, when it was offered to her, she was unable to accept it. The offer came at a bad time because her son, who had cystic fibrosis, was scheduled for a lung–heart transplant and she would not leave him. These reactions are all related to the timing of the transition. Clearly, Sue could not take advantage of her potential promotion because of her son's situation and Gail's father could not receive his pension because of his early death.

We sense we are off time by comparing ourselves with others in our age group. If it seems that all your friends are grandparents and you are not, or if all your friends' adult children have paying jobs and your children do not, you may think that something is wrong with your family. Being off time can create the most discomfort out of the four categories of transition, so you need to learn how to respond positively when the feeling arises. The following are some things you can do to ease the discomfort:

- Realize that feelings of failure can stem from being off time, but you are not a failure. You are merely off time according to a rigid formula you do not have to accept.

- Accept that there is no longer a "right time" to do things. Life is in flux, but we still hold to rigid ideas of appropriate behavior for different ages. And maybe that is the problem, maybe there is no single age that is "right" to go to school, to marry, or to retire. Today we live with conflicting realities. When good things happen to divert us from our life plans, they make us happy and we do not really feel off time. However, it can be confusing when we realize that our lives and futures are not predictable.

- Reset your social clock. We see people marrying in their 40s, becoming parents in their 40s, retiring in their late 50s, and changing careers in their 60s. Maybe we need to make our social clocks more flexible; after all, they are person-made. Returning to school at age 60 can be the right time for someone who never had a chance to finish a degree; divorcing at age 70 can be the right time for a couple who, after many years, have acknowledged their incompatibility; and inviting your adult child to return home after college can be a smart way to offer a base from which to get on a firm economic footing. There are no absolute rights or wrongs.

Out-of-Time Transitions

This is a state I have experienced personally. As my husband was dying, I had two major surgeries within 6 weeks; I was actually in a rehab center when my husband died. During that time, I felt completely disconnected from my normal life. I never looked at a newspaper, turned on the television, or read a book. For me, this served as a protected period that allowed me to grieve. I moved back into real time gradually, first with care at home, then with intense physical therapy, and my increasing determination to walk again. My experience was similar to that of Hagestad, who wrote that when she experienced a life-threatening illness, she basically lost track of the world outside and focused solely on getting well. Psychologist Erik Erikson also identified this phenomenon, calling it a *moratorium*, a time to explore your identity. That is exactly what I was doing—trying to figure out who I was after becoming a widow and having severe medical problems. For many of us, the way to cope with a transition is to take a time-out, to reset our identity and our clock.

No-Time Transitions or Nonevents

Nonevents are those transitions you expect but do not occur, because they are transitions that usually are not described in the literature. We rarely think of a baby, a relationship, or an expected promotion that did not materialize, as a major transition, yet it certainly changes your life in major ways. For example, Joan expected a happy life of family, career, and financial security. Instead, her first husband died when she was 35. She raised three children and remarried. Finally, her life was back on track, or so she thought. Then her son married and became a father of three children. After his wife became mentally ill, Joan's son became the sole guardian of his children. Joan found herself flying back and forth to her son's home to help care for the children. She is distressed about the crises but also about not living the life she expected as a "happy" retiree.

We all have dreams and expectations of what might have been. If you have not personally experienced a nonevent, someone in your family probably has. A graphic artist claimed that learning about nonevents made her better understand her father's relentless attempts to micromanage her business. "My father is a walking nonevent. He never had the promotions he expected and never made enough money to support his family. He was depressed and to compensate he tried to run my business."

In contrast to the other time-related conditions, nonevents are undercover, not celebrated or acknowledged. To learn more about how people understand and deal with challenges such as the marriage that never happened, the baby who never arrived, the promotion that never occurred, or the book that was never published, a team at the University of Maryland interviewed people of all ages about how nonevents changed their lives. We found that nonevents are not all the same, but that they differ in significant ways:

- Some nonevents are personal—Wanda was unable to lose the 50 pounds she gained since college; Harry could not afford to retire on time.

- Other nonevents, called *ripples*, stem from someone else's life—Lois is the only one in her crowd who was not a grandparent.
- Many nonevents are resultant, stemming from an event—Amy tore her tendon, which prevented her from engaging in physical activities.
- Other nonevents sometimes turn out simply to be delayed—You think you will never be a grandparent, and then your 45-year-old child has a baby; you think you will never marry, and at age 70 you find someone and marry for the first time.

If you are confronted with nonevents, you face two basic challenges: The first is to figure out when it is time to accept the reality that your dream is not happening; the second is to decide when to move on to Plan B. Successful coping requires many strategies, but my work shows that those who successfully have resolved these challenges have followed these four steps:

- Acknowledge the lost dream and make it public. For example, Don had always wanted to become a Navy pilot. "I was in the Navy and wanted to stay in, but my wife insisted I retire and continue with studying to be a lawyer. That is my big disappointment."
- Allow yourself to grieve for loss of the dream. Don is clearly grieving, because he can never really forget about his dream. Often grieving is public, but in the case of a lost dream, it is private. It is important to acknowledge that the process takes time—time to separate from the loss of a person or dream—then

face ambivalence about the loss, and eventually move forward. The process can take 6 months, a year, or more. There is no shortcut and no way to simply forget the loss.

- Reshape or modify the dream. Don exemplified this strategy by modifying his dream to still include opportunities to fly, even if just for fun. That decision allowed him to focus on making his career as a lawyer a satisfying one.

- Develop a ritual. For example, Martha did this when she sent an announcement to all her friends that she was no longer looking for Mr. Right and that they could find her place settings at Macy's. Similarly, Marcia, widowed for the second time, realized it was time to let go of the hope that she would find yet another life companion. Her ritual was joining three friends for a 3-day spa retreat to discuss what they had expected in life that did not occur and how to let go of their dreams.

According to Neugarten, "the psychology of the life cycle is not a psychology of crisis behavior or age so much as it is a psychology of timing."[3] Anyone born in the 20th century has experienced incredible changes in the space of just a few decades. As the context of our lives has changed, so must our personal concepts of age and time. At a recent Boomer Lifestyle Conference, the buzzword was *reinvention*. Why? Because according to Lorin Drake, a researcher who spoke at the conference, boomers are facing unprecedented detours from their traditional life goals. Drake said that 39% of Florida boomers had lost a job; another 34% had faced a health problem; 15% were dealing with mortgage problems; and 25% were living with parents or an adult child. One boomer was quoted as saying, "I did not sign up for this."

These numbers are, in a way, reassuring because they remind us that as we experience transitions, we are not alone; that transitions in and of themselves are a normal part of life.

The Transition Process

Perhaps the most difficult aspect of coping with a transition is accepting that it takes time. For the first few days, weeks, or months, you may think of yourself as a new graduate, a new widow, or a recent retiree—in every case, it is an identity that you did not have before. But with time, we can separate from the past to accept the changes and identify new niches where we will live our lives.

Exiting from a role is difficult. For example, Bill spent his 60s and 70s suffering an unrequited love. The woman he loved would sometimes encourage him, other times push him away. He was not able to leave her or exit from the relationship. Sara Lawrence-Lightfoot, author of *Exit: The Endings That Set Us Free* wrote, "We are free when we are able to exit from those forces and circumstances—the people, relationships, institutions, countries, ideologies, religions, ourselves—that hold us down or back . . . that limit . . . us."[4] Some people are unable to separate from their possessions, houses, or former identities.

As an example, the late Zandy Leibowitz and I studied 55 men whose jobs were eliminated at the NASA Space Flight Center in Goddard, Maryland. We interviewed them on the day their jobs were eliminated and followed up with another interview 6 months later. All but two of the men were devastated, saying things like, "The job loss was worse than a diagnosis of cancer." We fully expected to hear equally dire comments 6 months later. We were shocked when they all said things like, "If I can handle this, I can handle anything" and "Actually my life has taken a turn for the best." The difference was a result of an intervention NASA had implemented to help these men cope with their job loss. The men were assigned to a "buddy" who coached them until they found another job, either at NASA or in the larger community. This example shows that your reactions to any transition can change over time.

This is especially true if you experience a major transition, such as retirement or a death of a family member. You need to allow yourself time to grieve over the things that you will miss. You may experience a period of teetering between your old *roles*, *relationships*, *routines*, and *assumptions* and replacing them with new ones. How fast your new life emerges will depend on how much you anticipated and prepared for the change and the balance between your supports and your deficits.

YOUR TO-DO LIST

We need to acknowledge that change is an inevitable part of our lives. Fighting it will only make us unhappy. To make the best of change, we need to understand the dynamics of the process so that we can shape it to our advantage. Try the following exercises to analyze how you have handled life changes in the past, so you can improve your experience with future transitions.

To assist you in this task, consider the example of moving from your home with a yard, to a small apartment in a high-rise condo 3 miles away. Your role as homeowner gave you control over managing your physical home space; but by living in a condo, you are only one of many owners who make decisions about the building (e.g., painting the lobby, fixing the roof). Your close relationships with neighbors will be harder to maintain, and you will need to develop new ones. It will be difficult or impossible to continue the routine of a daily exercise walk in your previous neighborhood. Your assumptions about whom to call in an emergency will change when you acquire new neighbors and/or building staff.

Review the following dimensions that will make a difference in how you cope with change.

■ **Degree of change:** As you think about your move, think about a transition you have previously experienced—perhaps a job change, a move, or the shift to living on a retirement budget. Think about its effects on key aspects of your life, and rate yourself on how well you handled changes to each of the following using a 5-point scale (1 = *you failed;* 5 = *you aced it*).

■ *roles*
■ *relationships*
■ *routines*
■ *assumptions*

Anticipate a future transition—a health crisis for you or someone in your family, or the loss of your spouse or partner. Try to apply what you have learned from the previous exercise to figure out how you could handle your next transition, whether you can pinpoint it now or not. What would you do to enhance your control and respond positively to changes in each of these categories?

■ *roles*
■ *relationships*
■ *routines*
■ *assumptions*

■ **Timing:** Think about the timing of the transition in your life. Again using the 5-point scale, rate the difficulty of each of the following (1 = *very easy;* 5 = *very difficult*)

■ on-time transition (e.g., moving after you retire)
■ off-time transition (e.g., being forced to move after a job loss)
■ out-of-time transition (e.g., feeling disconnected to life, such as when you are ill)
■ nonevent (e.g., wanting to move but being unable to do so because of a physical or emotional problem)

- **Process:** Where are you in your transition? Have you begun to establish new *roles*, *relationships*, *routines*, and *assumptions*?

Now when you think about a transition, you can factor in the degree to which it changes your life, where you are in the transition process, and whether the timing was positive or negative. This understanding will help you embrace your transitions.

It can be difficult, even painful, to experience change. But avoiding it is not an option. Whether you are creating the transition or whether it comes as a surprise, your life will not be transition free. The basic question is how to embrace your transitions. The next chapter provides concrete coping strategies that you can carry with you all through life.

4

Diversify Your Coping Skills

The writer Roger Angell famously described his outlook on life at age 93 in an article for *The New Yorker* magazine titled "This Old Man: Life in the Nineties." He opened the article with a litany of his physical deficiencies, ranging from macular degeneration to stents in his arteries to nerve damage from shingles. He lost his dog, his wife, and a long list of friends, acquaintances, and family members who were not blessed with his longevity. He admitted that conversation sometimes becomes difficult, "full of holes and pauses," but he has figured out how to handle it: "I will pause meaningfully, duh, until something else comes to mind," he writes. "Here I am in a conversation . . . I chime in with a couple of sentences. The others look at me politely, then resume talk . . . What? Hello? Didn't I say something? . . . Yes, we are invisible." Yet, he declared, "I am 93 and I am feeling great. . . . I have endured a few knocks but missed worse. I know how lucky I am, and, secretly tap wood, greet the day and grab a sneaky pleasure from my survival at long odds."[1]

Despite the challenges of aging that he described, Angell has written and published a most articulate, affecting account of the transition to old age. The article title could have been "How to Cope With the Transitions of Aging," and been spot on. What Angell is doing in his 90s, in his own way, is using coping strategies that are available to all of us, without ever naming them.

As we have seen in the previous chapters, aging transitions come in many forms:

- Bev and Harry, both in their late 60s, excitedly moved to a new community with other transplants where Bev quickly became active in local civic affairs. Soon after they arrived, Harry had a stroke, and their lives were upended. Bev immediately became a caregiver, they stopped going out with friends, and they are trying to figure out how to make the most of their life despite the stroke.

- Nedya, a woman in her early 70s, just learned that her 50-year-old son is getting a divorce. She is very upset: "This is so unsettling. How will this affect my relationship with our daughter-in-law and grandchildren?"

- Stan, a caregiver for his 60-year-old spouse who is battling lung cancer, told me, "When you write your book, be sure to include depression, anger, and—most of all—helplessness." Stan is depressed. The thought of losing his lover and best friend of many years feels unbearable. Because they have family in their area, Stan occasionally is able to get out to meet with his social group, ROMEO (Retired Old Men Eating Out), but basically he stays tethered to his wife.

■ Sophia is simultaneously thrilled and upset. She is thrilled about becoming a great-grandmother. She offered to visit her son and daughter-in-law to help, but they have subtly indicated they think it would be too much for her. The implication is that she is too old, which upsets her.

What can we do when we face transitions that upset or overwhelm us? The one-word answer is simple: cope. But the exact answer differs for each individual because there is a myriad of strategies available.

BALANCE YOUR RESOURCES AND DEFICITS— THE 4 S SYSTEM

Your potential resources are clustered into four major categories, what I call the 4 S's: situation, self, supports, and strategies. No one factor alone will make the difference in how you handle the transition. What counts is the balance of your resources to deficits. For example, a retired couple was devastated at the loss of everything they owned after their house burned down. Their situation was negative—off the charts. Their biggest problem was their loss of identity. It took months for them to replace their driver's licenses and passports.

They had no way to prove who they were—no Social Security card or other official identification.

When they married, 10 years before the fire, the couple had been thrilled about the joining of their two families. Their adult children rallied around after the fire and gave them emotional and physical support. Two of their adult children decided to move back to the parents' community. The couple is very resilient. Although their situation was terrible, their self and supports were saving graces.

The couple also used many coping strategies. They kept counting their blessings that their 6-month-old grandchild was not visiting at the time and that no one was hurt. They reaffirmed that they would have the fun of building just the kind of house they wanted so all their children and grandchildren could visit. This couple was unusual but their experience illustrates that if the balance of resources to deficits is weighted toward more resources, you have a fighting chance to survive even the most terrible tragedy.

Here are the types of questions to ask yourself as you assess how to handle a particular transition.

- **Situation:** What is going on in your life at the time of change? Are there multiple stresses in your life? Is money a worry? Or is life fairly calm?
- **Self:** What are your inner resources? What are your personal strengths—things you do well that help you deal with change? For example, are you optimistic, resilient, and able to deal with ambiguity?

Think about how you have navigated transitions in the past.

- **Supports:** What people and activities can you count on for support during your transition? Think about which friends and family may be able to help you through the changes. Are there activities, interests, or hobbies (e.g., exercise, yoga, going to the movies, volunteering) that you can count on to provide solace and normalcy in your life?
- **Strategies:** Are you able to use a variety of coping strategies? (Read on to learn more about useful strategies.)

To illustrate the importance of striving for a balance between your resources and your deficits, consider the example of two individuals with the same disability—a torn abductor muscle in the hip. They cope in different ways depending on each person's ratio of positive resources to deficits. The first individual lives with her husband in a continuing care community. She has easy access to physical therapy, strong support on a daily basis from her husband and friends in the community, and a comfortable financial situation. The second individual lives alone, has limited finances, and is depressed. The negatives in this latter situation outweigh the positives. But fortunately, this individual finds a way to bolster her resources. She lives near a senior center. A friend helps her get to the center, where she starts making friends, participating in supervised exercise, and taking courses in creative coping.

WHAT IS COPING?

According to psychologists Richard Lazarus and Susan Folkman, *coping* occurs when the demands on a person exceed that person's resources for maintaining a stable life or routine. Lazarus and Folkman argued that it is not the specific event that makes the difference. Rather, it is how you look at it, how you appraise (a) the event or nonevent and (b) your resources for coping with it.

We are constantly coping with life's challenges—retirement, where to live, money, health, family relationships, and, of course, aging. As you look back over the years, you probably see times when you coped effectively and others when you fumbled.

Take the example of a woman who was offered a dream job, which required her moving to a new community, but turned it down because of a recent diagnosis of breast cancer. Her prognosis was good, but at the time she had to make the decision she felt she needed to remain in familiar surroundings and stay focused on fighting the cancer. Lazarus and Folkman quoted Hamlet: "There is nothing either good or bad, but thinking makes it so."[2]

Now comes the difficult part: how to cope creatively and effectively with whatever comes your way. The way we appraise the challenge will determine whether we tackle it with a problem-focused approach, an emotion-focused approach, or both. In the previous example of the older couple whose adult son is divorcing his wife, they are not able to use problem-solving coping because the decision of whether to get divorced or not is out of their hands. Rather, they must focus on their emotions. Why are they so upset? As we discussed in Chapter 3, transitions are upsetting because they change your life: your *roles*, your *relationships*, your *routines*, and your *assumptions*. Remember, even happy transitions can be stressful because so much is changed in your life.

YOUR COPING STRATEGIES QUESTIONS

Because there are hundreds of coping strategies, and hundreds of self-help books written about them, deciding which strategy to use can become a major challenge. You can be helped by looking at the work of sociologists Leonard Pearlin and Carmi Schooler, who interviewed 2,300 people between the ages of 18 and 65 to identify the major coping strategies people used as they faced life's strains and joys.[3]

They identified hundreds of strategies, categorized into the following groups, which are designed to do the following.

- **Change the situation:** This includes negotiating, seeking advice, brainstorming, and planning (what Lazarus and Folkman referred to as *problem-focused coping*).
- **Change the meaning of the challenge:** This includes developing rituals; relabeling or reframing; and using humor, resilience, and faith (what

Lazarus and Folkman referred to as *emotion-focused coping*).

- **Reduce your stress:** This includes playing, engaging in physical activity, going to therapy, reading, practicing mindfulness, listening to music, and engaging in spirituality.
- **Do nothing.**

When you face a challenge, ask yourself the following questions:

- Can I change the situation?
- Can I change the meaning of the situation?
- Can I relax?
- Or should I do nothing?

Take a look at some examples of how you might answer these questions.

How Can I Change the Situation?

There are many ways to change something you do not like or want. When faced with a transition—whether immediate or in the future (e.g., retirement), one strategy is to gain some control and confidence by consciously planning ahead.

Doris, an omelet cook at a restaurant, complained that her arm aches at night. She is looking forward to retirement, as the physical strain connected with her job is taking a toll on her. To cope with her current discomfort, she started thinking about what she wanted to do when she retires. From simply thinking about the future, she has since taken action by enrolling in a training program at the local children's hospital so that she can start volunteering as soon as she stops working.

Jim, another enthusiastic planner, started imagining what his future would look like several years before he planned to retire from a government agency. "I envision it as a time to reinvent myself; have time to lecture and write; mentor students in PR; learn how to cook, speak Spanish, and dance the tango; spend several weeks in a foreign city; read fiction; learn more about how to relax and be patient." Jim had also thought ahead about ways to keep in touch with his work colleagues and hoped to work 2 days a week as a consultant at his old agency, for at least the first year of his retirement.

Conventional wisdom suggests that planning ahead for education, marriage, family, career, retirement, or end-of-life decisions pays off. Even though none of us can read tea leaves, many of us believe that preparing for the future, though sometimes unsettling, is a necessary guide. But we must also acknowledge that our predictions may go astray.

Daniel Gilbert, a renowned Harvard University professor and author of *Stumbling on Happiness*, found that 12% of our daily thoughts are about the future; each of us is a "part-time resident of tomorrow." Despite that, Gilbert claimed that we are poor forecasters of our own futures.[4]

For example, when Joan and her husband, Jeff, were in their late 60s, she tried to convince him to sell their house and move to a small condo. When he refused, she said that she would move out if he died before her. When Jeff died at 75, Joan not only decided against moving, but she considered applying for a reverse mortgage so she could remain in their home. On a conscious level, she decided to remain in her home because of financial reasons and her dislike of institutional settings. In addition, she realized that she liked being alone in the house where she and her husband raised their children. She looked at retirement communities and hated the thought of living in one. What she previously thought about the future was not how she felt when the future became a reality.

In another example, doctors told Stew that he had become terminally ill after a 2-year struggle with congestive heart failure. He agreed to hospice care, as there was no hope of his getting better. After 6 months in hospice, Stew started asking his wife, doctor, and hospice team for more surgery despite having little hope of recovery. In his case, the doctors refused to operate so his change of mind was irrelevant. What is relevant is that what we think we will want in the future does not always turn out to be the case.

This might explain why some retirees migrate to warmer climates but later return to their original homes. They have not considered all the implications of the move, such as the high cost of living in the new community, missing long-time friends and family, or changes in their health and financial resources. "Planning requires that we peer into our futures, and anxiety is one of the reactions we may have when we do," according to Gilbert, because it is impossible to imagine every aspect of the future.

A focus group of baby boomers, organized as part of a PBS Pledge Special, *Retire Smart, Retire Happy*, confirmed the relationship between planning and anxiety. First, the baby boomers were scared that they might outlive their assets and, second, they were afraid that the future would probably involve caregiving. Several had observed many family and friends already in that role. Thinking about the future caused anxiety.

Sharing your concerns with others, whether family, friends, or professionals, can help. One couple started thinking about their financial future in their early 50s. They met with a financial planner who told them that they would need much less money in retirement, as they would have fewer needs for clothes and other material things. The wife looked the financial planner in the eye and asserted, "We will need more money, not less. We will travel more, buy clothes, and pay for fitness training. In addition, our health care costs will increase, and hopefully we will have grandchildren and we would want to help with their education."

Financial, medical, and psychological counselors, in many cases, can be helpful in planning for transitions. The previous example shows that the "expert" advice and the conventional wisdom do not always fit every individual. One might reasonably ask, "Should we avoid planning since we are poor forecasters?" Of course not. Planning ahead can help you focus on your situation, and then explore potential scenarios that otherwise may not have occurred to you.

How Can I Change the Meaning of the Challenge?

There are many times when life does not follow the script you intended. When you find yourself unable to change what is happening, this is the time to get out your kaleidoscope and consider reframing the situation—looking at what has happened in a new way. For example, I was due to make a speech in Denver, but as a result of a miscommunication with the organizer of the conference, I accidentally went a month early. I was very upset when I arrived at the hotel only to find it was scheduled for the following month. I was mad at myself, but luckily I could not attribute it to age because I was only in my 50s at the time. To help me cope, I went to lunch and wondered if any of my work could be of benefit. I thought my coping questions could guide me. I realized I could not change what had happened—I was in Denver in October instead of November—but I could change the way I looked at it. I could use my mistake as the opening for my talk when I returned the next month: "You have never had a speaker more eager to talk with you." Reframing can be an effective strategy.

When Beulah, a retired postal employee, realized she could not deal with her daughter's addiction, she changed the way she looked at the situation. Beulah saw the situation as an opportunity to raise her granddaughter and give her a stable life. By changing her perspective, she helped not only her granddaughter but also herself, by creating a vital, new, and rewarding purpose for her own life.

The character attribute that seems most important over the course of life is resilience. Sociologist Phyllis Moen suggested that after enduring a challenge or crisis, some people will return to a much less favorable state and others to their previous state, but in the best cases, people move forward and "sway the direction of their biographies."[5]

Will you be able to show resilience in the face of a major—or even a minor—crisis? We will all face circumstances, challenges, and opportunities requiring flexibility. It might be true that resilience is an inborn trait, but for those of us who need it and might not have it, it is comforting to know there are some strategies we can use to become more resilient.

Reframe Failure

Johnette was nominated to be on the national board of a major organization. The application and criteria were very challenging, but she was highly qualified. Secretly, she felt sure she would get appointed, so when she received the letter informing her that she was not selected, Johnette felt very disappointed, like a failure. But was she really a failure?

Erma Bombeck provided perspective for this discussion when she wrote,

> Failing is what most of us do . . . but we have still managed to go on breathing. . . . I have several reactions when I hear people introduce me [with] . . . accolades . . . so glowing that I do not even recognize myself. I figure Mother Teresa just flew in. . . . I would like to propose a new wrinkle to introductions. Instead of listing a speaker's successes, why not list [their] failures? "Born average, our guest tonight never rose above it. . . . Her first and last comedy album . . . raced to oblivion. . . . She has never won a Pulitzer Prize . . . [and] never been interviewed by Barbara Walters."[6]

And none of us would consider Erma Bombeck a failure.

In another example, the final speaker on a panel where 10 women were applauded for their successes said, "I want to speak about the failures each of us has had. We would not be standing before you if we had not faced failure. Remember that successful people have more failures than failures have."

So, if failing is something we all do, something we are all accomplished at, why fight it, why deny it? It is not failing that is the issue, but how we define it, cope with it, and grow from it. The following strategies show how you can put failure into perspective.

■ **Use failure to your advantage:** Retired Gen. Stanley McChrystal was forced to resign for inappropriate remarks he made that were critical of the White House. Did he fade away and disappear from public life? No. In fact, he lectures in a course on leadership at Yale University called "Coping With Failure."

- **Reframe and redefine failure:** Do not catastrophize. Realize that failing in one arena does not mean you are a total failure. Focus on what has been achieved, rather than on what has not been achieved.

- **Read about others' experience:** Carole Hyatt and Linda Gottlieb decided to write a book on failure, *When Smart People Fail*, after each had failed at a job. They interviewed hundreds of people who had been fired or experienced a failing career or marriage. The authors concluded, "There is no such thing as failure. Failure is the judgment of an event: the way you see loss of a job, the closing of a play."[7]

Reframe Aging

When you talk to anyone who is 50 or older, you will find their views of their own aging resurfacing at some point. They talk about the degree to which they feel their age and the degree to which their inner life and chronological age match. Here are a few examples.

Shauna and her partner, both in their early 70s, were pleased when they were able to secure the apartment they wanted in a retirement community. Soon after they moved in, Shauna had a rude awakening: "This is not me. I am a young, dynamic person inside and the walkers and wheelchairs do not fit my image. I said to my partner, 'we need to move out of here.'"

Six months later Shauna described her changing perspective. She was beginning to realize that she is not the young woman who inhabits her inner life. In fact, she is beginning to realize she is exactly where she belongs—in a community with lots of people ranging in age from 50 to 100. Even though she felt much too young to be among people with walkers and canes, over time she began to accept the fact that becoming chronologically old does not mean giving up. In fact, Shauna is still a beautiful, wise woman who is energetic and active. Part of being wise is accepting where you are in life, getting the most out of life, and staying involved.

Similar ambivalence about aging was evident during a conversation group with eight men and women in a community center, arranged by professional social worker Paula Falk. The diverse group included, among others, a former teacher, a former librarian, and a former housekeeper. When asked about their concerns, the first thing they mentioned was forgetfulness and memory loss. Paula pointed out that as you age it may be more difficult to multitask, and we may need to change the way we think. Instead of berating ourselves for memory loss, she suggested we say we now need to focus on one thing at a time.

Others mentioned that retirement has brought the joy of not having to punch a clock, of having the freedom to spend time as they want like going to church, meeting friends, and coming to the community center three or four times a week. One woman has taken up fishing with a passion.

They discussed using "big" birthdays as the perfect opportunity to honor a friend or relative. Probably more important, it is a time for the person experiencing the birthday to reflect not just on what has been lost, or on the new problems that have come with aging, but instead to think about what to do with the time they have left, to assess the opportunities to do something about one's regrets, and to think about the meaning of life. This would be a true example of reframing many of our most common attitudes and concerns about our own aging.

How Can I Minimize Stress?

Whether or not we are trying to alter what is going on or change the meaning of a particular situation, we need to use strategies that ease our stress. Some of the ways we can do this include using play and humor; practicing meditation and mindfulness; expressing emotions through praying, crying, laughing, and talking; and engaging in physical exercise like swimming, running, walking, tennis, and golf.

Recent attention has focused on the need to plan for play. Our society is so work oriented that people often do not build play into their lives. According to Dr. Stuart Brown, author of *Play: How It Shapes the Brain, Opens the Imagination, and Invigorates the Soul*, play is "spontaneous and allows for improvisation."[8] One woman said she crosses out 3 nights a week on the calendar so that she and her partner can make spontaneous plans to have fun. Think about it. Do you and others you know plan for playtime? Maybe it is time to start.

Practicing mindfulness has become a popular way of relaxing and reducing stress. Rezvan Ameli's book *25 Lessons in Mindfulness* provides a practical application that we can use as we attempt to eliminate some of the stresses in our life. "The essence of mindfulness is to pay attention to your present moment . . . to notice, to allow, and to observe what is happening in each moment with curiosity and openness."[9] Data are accumulating showing the positive effects of mindfulness on health and well-being. Meditation, one form of mindfulness, is an excellent way to focus and let go of negative emotions.

In *Love Is the New Currency*, Linda Commito shared the story of Sophia, who used her belief in God and her optimism to cope with the tragic, unexpected loss of her husband, Joey. Sophia was impressive in the way that she lived her life, with a positive outlook and an inspiring attitude that is downright contagious!

> I was the "girl from Harlem" who married the "Italian boy from the Lower East Side." We met while Joey was a hospital administrator at Bellevue Hospital Center and I was a volunteer. Our friendship, partnership, and love story developed into a beautiful marriage of 41 years.
>
> On the night before a presidential election, after waving signs and doing what we could to support [the nominee's] campaign, Joey was walking across University Parkway . . . when he was hit by a young driver who did not see him. Joey was thrown into the air, landing on his head, and as I looked at the blood coming from his

eyes and head, I knew that he was not going to make it. Despite the best efforts of the emergency team, he died before ever reaching the hospital.

Even while undergoing such personal loss and trauma, Sophia was able to reach deep within to offer comfort and compassion to the distraught young man who had killed her husband, saying, "Your car and you were in the wrong place at the wrong time. It was not your fault . . . it was God's destiny for him."

Speaking about her husband, she said, "Joey lived life to the fullest . . . he was happy, fulfilled, and had no regrets. There was no one for him to forgive, nor was there anyone who needed to forgive him." Sophia understood that special kind of unconditional accep-tance. She later wrote a caring letter to the young man involved in the accident to release him from any guilt, letting him know that there was nothing to forgive.

Sophia's spirituality allows her to believe that it was "time for God to take Joey home." God gave her this wonderful gift of a husband, and it was now time to return that gift. Several months later, Sophia said, "Joey's spirit and love surround me every day and I am blessed by God. Even with the loss of my husband . . . I still owe God big time!" She believed in doing what she could to repay those many blessings in her life.

Reflecting on her philosophy of life, Sophia stated that "in life, when one door closes, another door opens. You can elect to open it, close it, or pretend there is no door. I walk through all doors! I am always excited about what is on the other side!"[10]

Should I Do Nothing?

In one of the conversation groups I conducted, a man asked what is meant by "doing nothing" and another man answered, "It is a proactive stance. You decide not to choose." A woman commented that she had seen too many people out of work jump at the first job offer they received. They would have been better off doing nothing. Another woman mentioned her issue: She speaks what is on her mind to her husband without filtering it. Her husband suggested doing nothing before saying whatever she is thinking. He said he is open to discussing anything but believes in giving yourself a day or two to think things over. In other words, doing nothing does not necessarily mean you never do anything. Often it just means you postpone, delay, and give the issue some more thought before acting.

MANAGE MULTIPLE TRANSITIONS

Transitions do not always come in one neat, defined package. Sometimes one transition can lead to another, and we find ourselves needing multiple coping strategies.

Lucinda, a 57-year-old member of my conversation group at the YMCA, shared her story of multiple transitions. She and her husband experienced difficulties after they decided to move from the Midwest to Florida to care for her aging parents: "I was able to transfer [to Florida] and work from home. Everything looked like it was working out. After 6 weeks, I received a notice from my company that my job was being eliminated."

She took advantage of her 6-month severance package, which included salary, health care, and access to outplacement coaching services. When they had initially moved, her husband had taken a job that he did not like, which he decided to leave. Once the 6 months ended, they started living on savings. In addition to the financial challenges, they were new to the community and had no local support system.

At the same time she was forced to retire, Linda had moved to a new community. So she was dealing with multiple losses, as well as trying to reestablish her *roles*, *relationships*, *routines*, and *assumptions*. She experienced the transitions of a geographical move (her choice), a new role as caregiver (her choice), and a job loss for her and her husband (not her choice), which led to a subsequent loss of income. The results were financial problems and loss of supports.

Using the 4 S's we can look at Lucinda's assets as she struggled to negotiate multiple transitions. Her situation went from very positive in her previous job and community to terrible in her new community. Her supports after she moved were nonexistent, but now she is doing something about that. In general, she is very positive. She gets discouraged but then takes action. She uses lots of strategies flexibly. Admitting to a period of self-pity when hit by all these transitions, Lucinda explained she just made up her mind to cope and "just do it." She read the local paper with a fine-toothed comb and discovered a group called Stakeholders in Aging. She attended a meeting, met people, and began networking. As a result, she was offered a consulting job with a coaching organization, a job that had potential for becoming long term. Her husband developed a consulting business they hope will become a full-time job.

Although both are on paths to more permanent work, they continue to face financial challenges.

> We analyzed our budget and stripped out anything that was not essential (e.g., hiring out yard work, dining out, clothes shopping). Although we have always been frugal, we took it to a new level and it is likely we will be living off our savings for the foreseeable future while we each get our respective businesses off the ground this coming year. It is not a complaint, just a realistic view of things.

For stress reduction, Lucinda decided to return to her love of horseback riding—a pleasure she had given up when they moved. This is her one extravagance. Through this activity, she is making new friends with women who share her interest.

YOUR TO-DO LIST

Now it is your turn. Choose a transition you experienced previously or one that you are facing now. As you think about your resources for coping with your transition, mark which ones need strengthening. The Transition Guide is a self-scoring guide that you can take to help you asses your transition and your resources for coping with it.[11]

- Is the situation in your life a good one or a bad one?
- Do you have a strong self? Are you a resource, an optimist, or a resilient person?
- Do you have sufficient support as you cope?
- Are you able to choose from and use a variety of coping strategies?

Remember that there is no single, magic-bullet coping strategy we can use in every situation. You need to assess whether you want to and can change what is challenging you. If you cannot change it, reframe it. And no matter what, use relaxation strategies to minimize the stress. In other words, the strategies you use depend on your particular situation. It is important to remember that there are many strategies available to you—and that creative coping means using strategies flexibly. If one strategy does not work, there are many others you can try.

III

NAVIGATE THE MANY TRANSITIONS OF AGING

5

Create Your Own Retirement Fantasy

At the age of 75, Ann retired from working as a certified nursing assistant. She loved taking care of physically challenged people; she felt connected to her clients and she had a purpose in life. This was Ann's second retirement, the one she planned for after retiring 15 years earlier from managing a physicians' practice. She knew that now she wanted to take some time for herself, time to have more fun and more freedom, away from the pressures of a job. So she planned on taking a break, a moratorium, time to think about and plan what she would do next.

Molly's retirement experience differed greatly from Ann's. In the sense of a finite date, her retirement was planned, but figuring out what to do next took a lot longer. Her decision to set a date for retiring from the bank had come to her one day as she was leaving a retirement party for an older colleague. She heard a number of comments indicating that her colleague should have retired several years ago, despite the fact that she was still an active, productive person. Molly thought,

> I knew right then that I would retire before I "needed" to—that I never wanted anyone to say that about me. And after many discussions with my supervisor, I retired at 68. I was not worried; after all, I had years of experience that led me to believe that I would ace retirement. But how wrong I was!

Rob retired at age 68 with no interest in ever working again. He moved into golf, fishing, and other leisure pursuits.

Soon after Nancy retired, a newspaper reporter interviewed her about a project she had directed. He asked her a simple question: "How do you want to be identified in this story? What is your title?" Nancy almost gagged and could not get out the words "I am retired." She fudged and said something like "I am a consultant." Several months later, as she was on her way out the door of her apartment, her retired husband asked: "Where are you going? When will you be back?" This also came as a shock, as Nancy had worked all her married life and was not used to reporting in to someone. Her dilemma of adjusting to retirement was further intensified when friends asked, "Now that you are retired, what will you do?"

It was evident in these examples that some people are uncomfortable with this uncharted territory and that they should have learned more about the retirement transition. The more they struggled to define their retirement, the more it became clear that we are living in a period when the very definition of retirement is changing. It is tempting to equate retirement with aging, but this is not always accurate. For people in some fields—pilots, professional athletes, dancers, or military personnel—retirement comes at an early age. For them, retirement may involve a whole new career, or starting a new business. Homemakers also face retirement issues when their kids go off to college, and their role changes drastically. They too face the daunting task of constructing a new life.

After my own retirement from a university, I decided that my next project would be a personal one: I would study retirement as a way to understand more clearly what I was experiencing and then share this understanding with others in the same boat. From that work, four key insights emerged that helped me adjust to this new phase of life—insights I hope will help you create your own path to a happy retirement.[1]

- Retirement is not just one date on the calendar; it is a series of transitions.
- Retirees need a strong *psychological portfolio* (discussed later in this chapter), as well as a financial one.
- Retirees decide which path to follow.
- Retirees dream about their future.

RETIREMENT IS A SERIES OF TRANSITIONS, NOT A DATE

Sociologist Phyllis Moen suggested that people spend more time planning a wedding than planning for retirement, and both events have a great deal in common.

There is a wedding date and a retirement date. What is often neglected is planning for what happens next. You plan for a wedding but not the marriage; you plan for retirement but not for the years after. Both are major transitions and not events at one point in time.

Studies of people in transition show clearly that transitions do not happen at one point in time. They are a gradual process. Although the onset of a transition may be linked to one identifiable event, the entire process may take 6 months, 1 year, or even 2 years. Transitions take time, and people's reactions to them change—for better or worse—while they are underway. In the first phase, we may think only about being a new grandfather, a new widow, or a recent retiree. This is frequently followed by a middle period of disruption— a period of confusion. In retirement, this is the time when you leave the structured world of work but have not yet gotten into a new life without work as you knew it. You might go through a period of wondering when it will end and when you can get on with your life. If, for example, you have just retired, what do you do? How do you dress? What does it feel like to lose the inter-action with colleagues on work tasks and in informal moments, such as coffee breaks? In the final phase, the change becomes integrated into your life, for better or worse. You have accommodated to your transition. Only then can you really separate from the past and move toward a new *role*, new *relationships*, new *routines*, and emerging *assumptions* about yourself and the world.

Of course, each person's experience is unique, and people do not move in lockstep through these three phases. Some people move from work life to retired life very quickly. For example, a retired reporter from a major newspaper had carefully planned his retirement. He was a Sunday painter and decided to become a serious artist. He fixed up his garage as his studio, and the day after he left the paper he started working there. A year later, he reported that he was very happy but would not call himself a painter until he had a show in a gallery.

In another example, a retired public school administrator found his first month of retirement very difficult as he was accustomed to his routine, his relationships, and his professional identity, all of which he missed in his postwork life. A year later, he had established a new life. He participated in an exercise program, volunteered for the court system as a guardian ad litem, and was becoming active with the League of Women Voters. It took some trial and error, but he found the right combination for himself.

We have seen that planning ahead can sometimes be problematic, and negotiating transitions can be tricky. However, knowledge about the process can alleviate the confusing feelings that often accompany transitions.

RETIREES NEED A STRONG PSYCHOLOGICAL PORTFOLIO

The term *psychological portfolio* emerged after I interviewed a number of retirees. They constantly described the challenges of finding a new life after retirement.

They inevitably discussed the challenge to their identity, the loss of no longer having a purpose, and the changes in their relationships. They described the challenges of finding a new life after retirement. Their comments revolved around the three components: their emerging identity, their personal relationships with friends and family, and their finding new purpose in life. Financial advisors commonly recommend that your financial portfolio contain three main types of assets: stocks, bonds, and cash. Similarly, you can also think about identity, relationships, and purpose as retirement assets in your psychological portfolio. Analyze their strength in your current portfolio, and then focus on how you can build on them to enhance and enrich your life as a retiree. Ideally the three components of your portfolio should all be strong, and of equal strength.

- **Identity:** What do you put on a calling card? How do you identify yourself when you meet someone? Modifying or changing your identity as circumstances change requires resilience. Incorporating a new identity takes time. Meanwhile, though, it is important to remind yourself that you are more than your former job title. Over time, as you develop new roles, relationships, and routines, your new identity will solidify.
- **Relationships:** The quality and number of our social connections, whether with family, friends, colleagues, or neighbors, can make a big difference in satisfaction with our daily life. Replacing work

relationships can take time and requires effort. Many retirees have commented that they do not miss work, they miss the schmoozing. It is critical to find a substitute for work relationships. Readjusting family relationships, especially adjusting to spending more time with your spouse or partner, can also be challenging. Cal, a retired executive with no purpose or agenda, began shopping with his wife at the supermarket. He was amazed at himself when he argued at the checkout counter about the brand of cereal his wife had selected. He began to realize he needed a purpose. Another couple felt guilty about wanting to spend their retirement sailing and having adventures when their daughter had hoped they would help with child care.

- **Purpose:** What makes you want to get up in the morning? Many retirees complain that after work their days are empty. One woman said, "When I worked I helped companies figure out their mission. Now that I am retired, I need someone to help me figure out my mission." Sociologists Phyllis Moen and Vivian Fields concluded that work provides social as well as financial capital.[2] After retirement, one way to replace the lost social capital is to volunteer or to work part time. Many studies have found that volunteering can enhance mental health and even longevity. But volunteering presents a conundrum—after working hard at a job, it feels demeaning to be asked to return to volunteering. According to a report, *The New Volunteer Workforce*, nonprofit organizations desperately need volunteers; yet every year volunteers leave their posts in growing numbers. To stem this tide, the report included as one of its suggestions a hybrid plan of providing stipends for volunteers.[3] One woman resented volunteering because she was doing many things she used to do as a professional but receiving no pay. She felt guilty and asked, "Wasn't this the time to give back, to feel grateful for all that I had received over my life?" Then something amazing happened that changed her perspective. She was invited to work on a short-term project at the Senior Friendship Centers as a "workateer," where she was offered a small amount of money. According to Dennis Stover, then-vice president of Senior Friendship Centers, workateering is a concept that bridges the experienced worker to the volunteer role and adds value and benefit to what volunteers are providing to organizations. A small stipend is paid for the work the volunteer does. It is work with some dollars attached that helps the person with a past work-life begin a life in which his or her talents are connected mostly to volunteering. Stover expressed the hope that this hybrid concept adds to the discussion of how we approach volunteerism as the baby boomers retire and seek purpose in their next life phase. A professional writer expressed similar sentiments: "I do not want to do writing assignments for no pay. The issue is that I have credentials and do not want to be treated as someone who does not have them."

Retirees Decide Which Path to Follow

Even before you retire, you should analyze your psychological portfolio. You can ask yourself, "What will be my retirement identity? How are my relationships likely to change? What will be my new sense of purpose?" If you are already retired, you can pose similar questions: "Have I created a new identity? Have I forged new and satisfying relationships? Have I found a purpose for my postwork life?"

Regardless of where you are in the retirement planning process, to recharge your portfolio, it might be time to think about your future path. Through my research, I have identified six major paths retirees follow. It is important to note that a path may not always be a straight line. People change paths, combine paths, and pursue paths in their own unique way. You can identify yourself by the type of path you choose.

■ *Continuers* modify their activities while continuing along a similar path. A retired teacher identified as a continuer: "I continue writing and speaking but no longer teach or work for an organization. As my daughter said, 'The only thing retired about you is your paycheck.'" Continuers maintain their former identity but in a modified way. Mort, a retired museum director, occasionally curates an art show. Larry, a retired roofer, will help out his old firm in an emergency. Continuers stay connected to their former work and their former identities while developing on new fronts.

- *Adventurers* see retirement as an opportunity to pursue an unrealized dream or try something new. Jane, a retired teacher, turned her hobby of raising goats into her new life. She bought a small farm and raises angora goats. She is making yarn and selling it at craft fairs. When Linda's job was eliminated and she was forced into retirement, she needed to reinvent herself. She was hired by a start-up nonprofit organization, now is learning about the field and is enjoying the challenge. She is adventuring into a new world.

  Marc Freedman, author of the book *Encore: Finding Work That Matters in the Second Half of Life*, started a movement called Encore Careers, which is intended to stimulate daydreaming and encourage adventuring into something new, maybe into something one had never thought of before.[4]

- *Easy gliders* have worked all their lives and decided that retirement is the time to relax. They take each day as it comes. Sam, a retired bank teller, now plays golf and poker and babysits for his grandchildren. For some, the joy of having no agenda and no pressure makes for a relaxed and rewarding life.

- *Involved spectators* still care deeply about their previous work. They are no longer players, but they receive satisfaction from staying involved. For example, Steve, a retired lobbyist, is no longer physically able to walk the halls of Congress, but he still follows the news and stays on top of current events.

- *Searchers* are retirees who are looking for their niche. At some point, any of us may be a searcher.

We might retire, then adventure into a new path, and then when that has played out, we might search again. Think of all the times you have asked yourself, "What's next?" Searchers try out new activities during this trial-and-error period. Searchers and adventurers are similar but not the same. Searchers keep looking, Adventurers are actually doing something new and different. The searcher might end up becoming an easy glider, an involved spectator, or an adventurer.

- *Retreaters* come in two versions. Some step back and disengage from their previous routine, using a moratorium to figure out what is next. Others get depressed and become couch potatoes.

You can ask yourself which path you want to pursue. You can follow any path or a combination of paths. After a retirement workshop, a woman told me, "When people used to ask me what I was doing now that I am retired, I said fliply, 'I am not dead yet.' Now I will say, 'I am an involved spectator.'"

RETIREES DREAM ABOUT THEIR FUTURE

We all know the phrase "What do you want to do when you grow up?" This question looms large as one approaches retirement. In my conversation groups, one woman fantasized about selling clothes in an upscale dress shop, a former Navy pilot dreamt of owning a plane and flying to visit his children who were in scattered locations, another woman imagined owning a book store, and one of the men saw himself working in Third World countries.

Structuring your retirement life around a fantasy, such as owning a plane, is really *reinvention*—a term that has increasingly been used by popular writers and experts to suggest embarking on a brand new life path. Making a fantasy a reality usually requires a lot more than just articulating it, and a lot more than luck.

But the question is, can we really reinvent ourselves? Perhaps it is better to think about change along a continuum. One end of the continuum is your current life and your life experience, the middle of the continuum may mean going to Plan B, and the other end of the continuum includes changing your life dramatically.

When Bob, who worked on a research project for the government, lost his job at age 63, he was clearly despondent. He took a 2-week sailing trip alone to reflect about his life. He remembered how massage therapy helped him when his first wife died at an early age. He wanted to help people as he had been helped, so he decided to become a massage therapist. This was, indeed, a radical change from the suit-and-tie life he had lived. His friends were shocked, but Bob knew what he wanted. He enjoyed his training and new work. After her initial surprise, Bob's wife became proud of him for following his dream. Whatever path you follow, you need to take account of the financial implications. In Bob's case, he had moved from a high-paying, high-level job to a job with much less money and prestige.

He and his wife had many discussions about whether her work could help support them during his training period.

THE MONEY ANGLE

For most Americans, one of the most important factors in making retirement decisions is their financial status. The amount of income you will receive in retirement affects setting a retirement date and the quality of life you will be able to enjoy once you leave the workforce.

A 2015 study by the National Council on Aging found that three of the top worries of Americans age 60 and over related to financial issues: financial security, sudden bills, and cutting costs.[5] This is understandable because it is almost inevitable that aging and retirement comes with lower income. According to 2014 U.S. Census figures, the median household income was $54,462. For those ages 55 to 64, it was slightly above the median: $61,471. But for the group over 65, the figure was much less: $37,907.[6]

A reduction in income can have serious consequences—including a decline in your daily quality of life and inability to meet unexpected financial needs, such as health care—that you need to be aware of before you set a retirement date. To minimize or avoid financial shocks in retirement, more and more of us are working beyond age 65, which has long been considered the "traditional" retirement age. We find that older Americans are working more today than they did in the past. There are people who will say they will never retire and go on to follow one of the more aggressive paths described earlier in this chapter. The trends toward living longer, and healthier, also may contribute to this elongation of work years. But we also know that some people have extended their working life not because they love their job but for purely financial reasons: As long as you continue to work, chances are you will accumulate more savings and be able put off spending the money you already have saved.

Whether you are planning retirement or are already there, the challenge is the same: To make sure that your income from various sources is adequate to (a) meet your basic needs and (b) provide "extras," such as travel, moving to a new home, or legacies for grandchildren. Success begins with planning, knowing how much income you can count on from Social Security, other pensions, savings, and investments, if you draw them down at certain ages. The date you choose to start Social Security, or to withdraw from a 401(k), for example, can make a big difference not only in the amount of income you receive but also in the size of your tax bill. If you withdraw too soon, you may incur penalties. Once you have pinned down the income data, you will need to come up with a realistic budget and make decisions about how to ensure your income will cover the budget. This process applies even to those who are already retired, who should continue to do an annual financial checkup to make sure that they are still on track.

Your retirement should be a happy time, a time when you have the security and flexibility to make your own schedule and to choose your own activities, companions, and location, free of anxiety about money.

This is why I have put getting your finances in order as a top priority on this chapter's to-do list.

YOUR TO-DO LIST

It is important to realize that creating a happy retirement does not necessarily require that you make radical changes in everything about your life. Acknowledging that the unexpected may always be lurking just out of sight, there are some follow-up steps you can take to move toward your retirement fantasy.

- **Secure your financial situation:** I hope you will be doing this long before you stop working, but without financial security, your retirement options will be very limited. As you get closer to retirement, do a thorough checkup each year, with professional help if possible, to make sure you are on track. Through the checkup process, you should make specific calculations of your retirement income and expenses. Then, as you are still working, make adjustments that will improve your ability to respond to financial challenges in retirement.
- **Study retirement before it happens to you:** Community colleges and other local organizations, such as the YWCA or YMCA, often offer low-cost, usually short-term courses, seminars, or other

events on how to approach retirement planning. Attending such sessions can help you start thinking about your options as well as your financial plans. (A note of caution: Be extremely wary of "retirement planning" events sponsored by financial organizations and companies that are mostly interested in selling you annuities, securities, or other financial instruments that may be fraudulent or inappropriate for you.)

- **Be open to chance encounters that might provide the clue for your happiness:** Professor John Krumboltz has been studying the role of happenstance as our careers unfold. His book, *Luck Is No Accident: Making the Most of Happenstance in Your Life and Career*, points out the importance of taking advantage of chance and of making the most of luck.[7]
- **Explore the path you want to take:** Do you want to be a continuer, adventurer, searcher, involved spectator, easy glider, retreater, or some combination?
- **Dream a little:** What have you always wanted to do? This is your chance to think about what you have always wanted to do to create a life after retirement that is rich and rewarding.

It is easy to view retirement as a loss. When we lose our job and/or our career, we can lose our routines, our relationships, our role, and our assumptions. In the most basic sense, retirement is a loss of work. The challenge is to replace what we have lost, if possible, with something that is even better. For some people, such as Ann, who had a second career as a nurse, retirement may mean taking on a different type of work. For retirees who do not want other work in the traditional sense, there are many opportunities, from spending time with grandchildren to learning how to knit to volunteering at a homeless shelter.

Like any other time of life, in retirement, the best-laid plans can go awry; surprises, good and bad, can occur at any time. But that does not mean you should avoid thinking about the future. What will matter most, ultimately, is your own personality, your ability to be resilient and optimistic, to be curious, to take initiative, and to build on what you have learned over the decades. That is how you will create a satisfying retirement, regardless of whether it is exactly the one you plan.

6

Choose Your Place:
Location, Location, Location

Mary, a 72-year-old widow whose disabled adult child lives with her, is trying to figure out her plan for the future. She is constantly reviewing her choices. She wonders,

> Should I move into a small apartment in a retirement community? Should I delay the move for a few years? Would I be causing harm to my daughter, because the move would force the issue of her moving out on her own?

Mary's answers to these questions vary from one day to the next, and so far, she has taken no action.

As we age, it is common for transitions in our life (e.g., retirement, changes in health or financial status) to lead us to think about whether to move.

A women's group met for years to talk about children, in-laws, husbands, careers, among other things. By the time they were in their 60s and 70s, they began to discuss when to retire and what to do after they had

107

retired. In their 70s and 80s, the talk often shifted to where to live. Should they move into a retirement community? Should they make their homes user-friendly and safe? Should they move closer to their children?

My first transition study centered on geographical moving. Although it might seem to be an ordinary part of life, relocating can have extraordinary consequences. Even if you just move across town, your routines change, like stopping for coffee or dropping off dry cleaning. If you relocate to a new job and new city, almost everything changes—your *role, relationships, routines*, and *assumptions*. This initial study helped identify these and other factors that make a difference as you cope with any transition.

While writing this book I made a major move, presumably my last. I had an epiphany one night—it was finally time to move to a retirement community. I had been resisting this for several years, and when I announced this to my partner, he said, "We are not ready yet." But if we were not ready at 86 and 89, when would we be ready? Friends asked how I could leave my wonderful apartment. My answer was that I need to walk the walk. I have promoted the importance of being engaged with others, and there is a better chance to stay engaged living in a community of people of similar age dealing with similar issues. Because I am in good physical shape, I was interested in a community that has activities, as well as many services. I was also interested in a community where some of the initial deposit would be returned. Of course, the move was not a clear-cut decision. One change it implied was giving up an apartment in a condo with many ages represented. But in making the move to a retirement community, I was really projecting my future needs when I might need physical and medical help. I have found, in my research and my personal experience, that location matters.

LOCATION MATTERS!

Malcolm Gladwell told an informative story in the introduction to his book *Outliers: The Story of Success*, about Stewart, a physician, who discovered a town where "there was no suicide, no alcoholism, no drug addiction, and very little crime." The physician compared the town, Roseta, with nearby towns with the same demographics. In Roseta, there was a "powerful, protective social structure." People talked to each other and had three generations under one roof. There was constant caring and interaction. Stewart was convinced that the place you live could affect your health and life.[1]

In his book, *Shock of Gray*, Ted C. Fishman compared Rockford, Illinois, with Sarasota, Florida. In Rockford, he wrote, people felt and acted old when they were 50. People left Rockford, whereas people from everywhere came to Sarasota. He concluded that "in Sarasota, the 60-year-olds are the 'kids,' whereas in Rockford, the 50-year-olds . . . are getting on."[2]

In a report in the business section of the *New York Times*, the author compared Fairfax County, Virginia, where the median household income is $107,000, with McDowell County, West Virginia, where the income is about $21,000.³ Whether you live in a town of "haves" or "have-nots" ultimately may affect your life expectancy. The report said that in Fairfax County average life expectancy is 82 for men and 85 for women, whereas in McDowell County it is 64 for men and 73 for women.

All of these reports tell us that where we live makes an enormous difference. Although access to a healthful environment and health care may promote greater longevity and even happiness, these are only some of the criteria to take into consideration as you think about moving. Cost of living, climate, proximity to family and friends, access to social life, and access to community services, such as public transportation, are only a few of the many factors to analyze before you make a decision to move. Maybe we should change the mantra "Age in place" to "Age in the location that will promote fun and friends."

LOCATION OPTIONS

Before we became a mobile society and lived so long, there were few location options available for aging people. Our parents, grandparents, and other ancestors usually stayed in the family home, often with care from children or other family members. If they became seriously ill or disabled and the family could afford it, they moved to "an old age home." In most cases, people did not have the luxury of choosing to relocate because they would prefer a better climate, or a less costly environment, or proximity to better health care facilities.

Now, as options have multiplied, the location decision has become much more complex. Beth Baker's award winning book, *With a Little Help From Our Friends: Creating Community as We Grow Older*, described innovative approaches to living with a clear focus on the importance of living in a community with social support, "people . . . are creating ways to live in a community, alternatives that give them more control, more companionship, more dignity, and more choice."[4]

For older people at the low end of the income spectrum, the amount of available income may be the major factor in determining where they live; they may have few or no choices. According to Steve Protulis, president and CEO of Elderly Housing Development and Operations Corp., money has been taken away from some of the government program options for low-income individuals, reducing the availability of housing. Consider the case of Gerry, who had to figure out where to live with no financial resources of her own. Her troubled marriage had ended in divorce, after which she moved to a small Midwestern town to live with her former mother- and father-in-law. She has no money because she has been unable to work as a result of emotional issues. Therefore, she pays no rent to her in-laws, who own a boarding house, but at times tries to help out her mother-in-law. Three families live in one house—her in-laws, her brother-in-law and his family, and Gerry. Her ex-husband lives in a nearby boarding house also owned by her in-laws. She feels fortunate that she was able to create a livable option for herself.

Once you have a clear understanding of the location criteria that are important to you, you will have choices from one of three major categories of options: (a) age in place, (b) remain in your current community but move to another living situation (e.g., another house or apartment, assisted living or cohousing), or (c) move to a different geographical area.

Age in Place

The Joint Center for Housing Studies at Harvard University reported that over 75% of people over 80 live in their homes. Remaining in your current home is particularly appealing if your mortgage is paid off and if the money you would make on the sale of the house would not cover the cost of other options. Some stay in their home because they simply cannot afford to leave. However, without some type of support, aging in place may not be the best option. An article in *JAMA Internal Medicine* noted that "15.6% of the elderly, community-dwelling Medicare population (approximately 2 million people) was completely or mostly homebound in 2011."[5] Your ability to stay in your home may require access to services or assistance, as well as physical repairs to make it safer. In some areas, these needs have given rise to the concept of *villages*–networks of residents who provide volunteer assistance to their neighbors for tasks such as trips to the doctor, shopping, or minor home repairs. The concept originated with the Beacon Hill neighborhood of Boston in 2002 and has proliferated into an estimated 150 villages in the United States and dozens more overseas. Members usually pay an annual fee (several hundred dollars is common) to hire staff to organize the services and social events and vet volunteers. The concept has become so popular that in Washington, DC, alone, there are some 14 villages.

Another way to age in place is to share your home. For example, three women who live in Gaithersburg, Maryland, have shared a home since they started their careers in Washington, DC, in the 1960s. Advantages include sharing expenses, regular social contact, and the comfort of knowing someone is nearby in an emergency.

Older people who have a very limited income face difficult challenges in finding an appropriate residence. Sometimes the answer is government-subsidized housing. A good place to start your search is the website of the U.S. Department of Housing and Urban Development (http://portal.hud.gov/hudportal/HUD?src=/program_offices/fair_housing_equal_opp/seniors). There are a number of possible programs for affordable housing. Unfortunately, locating and ultimately finding such opportunities can be a time-consuming process, so if you anticipate needing this type of housing, the best advice is to do your research early.

Move Within Your Community

Options in this category may include cohousing, living in a village, and/or a life plan community (formerly designated continuing care retirement community).

■ **Villages:** Some projects that call themselves *villages* are actually *cohousing*, or residential clusters created to promote a sense of community and shared responsibility among the residents. They usually include some communal facilities, such as a dining and activities area, and have some form of group governance.

■ **Retirement community:** Many living in a retirement community are enthusiastic about explaining how much they like being part of a community of like-minded people with many activities and restaurants on the premises. Of course, there are exceptions. Georgia, a 75-year-old woman who had put a deposit on a retirement community in a major urban area, has another take on it. After visiting it a number of times, she changed her mind, cancelled her deposit, and rented an apartment in a large apartment building with residents of all age groups. As she said, "In my new neighborhood, there is activity on the street and in the building. In addition, it is near a subway and many restaurants. In other words, there is no one size that fits all." Many express just the opposite opinion. One man expressed it this way: "I feel safe. In addition I like the social activities."

- **Life plan community:** The advantage of this type of arrangement is that you can stay on one campus, moving to different residential models, as your needs change. The AARP defined this option as "part independent living, part assisted living, and part skilled nursing home, and [life plan communities] offer a tiered approach to the aging process, accommodating residents' changing needs."[6] Entering such a community, especially at the independent living level, may offer a sense of security and knowledge for you and your family that you will have access to needed care in the future. The downside for many people is the cost: an initial investment that the AARP says ranges from $100,000 to a million dollars, plus several thousands of dollars per month in fees.

Relocate to a New Geographical Area

Enabled by the new mobility of our environment, the nation's 77 million baby boomers are reconsidering their housing needs and making changes as they become "empty nesters."

Moving to a warm climate may attract many, but climate needs to be considered along with other criteria. Each year, various researchers and publications come up with lists of "the best" places to retire and they are by no means all in warm climates. *Forbes* Magazine, for example, offered a list of best retirement venues in 2015 that included towns and cities in Idaho,

Wyoming, Pennsylvania, and North Dakota, as well as others in the Sun Belt.[7]

Separating from roots and routines in your current community, regardless of how long you have lived there, is a big decision that should be based on some serious thinking about how you imagine living your later years, your relationship to your family, whether you have friends in the new location, and your current and future health status. Once you have decided you definitely want to leave your current base, you will need to figure out whether it makes sense to rent or to buy a property; then sort through the types of residential options previously described.

Although there are no reliable statistics, it appears that an increasing number of Americans are spending or considering spending their retirement years in another country. As with states and localities in the United States, various research groups also issue regular reports on the best countries for overseas retirement.

A couple, an artist and a writer, wanted to find an overseas retirement locale offering an affordable but high-quality lifestyle, a good climate and access to affordable care if they developed infirmities as they aged. They lived in Spain for a while, learned the language, and became comfortable in the Latin culture. In their 60s, they moved to South America and opened a bed and breakfast and tour business, thinking they would make their permanent home there. But after nearly a decade of part-time residence, they decided against it, on the basis of political and economic uncertainties and the challenge of truly integrating into the society. Now in their 70s, they are back living in the United States in their original home—which they never sold—and trying to figure out next steps. They still visit South America, where they have friends, but they know that in the future the long airplane trip may prove too much for them.

UNDERSTAND THE RELOCATION TRANSITION

As you consider where to live, you need to pay special attention to four issues that may have a major impact on your location decision: (a) your struggle to decide, (b) your sense of control, (c) your identity, and (d) your happiness.

Your Struggle to Decide

What to do? How to plan the last third of your life? As noted in Chapter 4, Daniel Gilbert warned that we are poor forecasters of our futures. For example, an 85-year-old woman with limited income has fallen several times, once breaking her pelvis and then her hip. For years she has tried to figure out where to move. The retirement communities she liked were not affordable. She tried to imagine what she would do if she became disabled. Her son and daughter-in-law have encouraged her to move to New York City, where they live. For years she has been saying she must decide. The problem is partly financial, partly inertia, and partly that she likes where she is now. It is not an easy decision.

In another example, Stella and her husband, Nick, found the decision to move was complicated by the fact that Nick was ill. They decided it would be better to move to a continuing care community. They put their apartment up for sale and selected an apartment in the new community. Just as they were getting ready to finalize the purchase, Nick's doctor told them he was too ill to move. They cancelled everything, deciding to stay put and hire helpers. Within a year, Nick died, and 2 years later Stella moved into the community she had originally selected.

There is no magic way to make the "right" decision. There needs to be flexibility to accommodate your changing conditions and needs. Talking with financial and psychological counselors can help clarify your decision.

Your Control of the Transition

How much control do you actually have over where to live? There are two kinds of control: your ability to influence life circumstances and, when that is not possible, your ability to control how you manage the circumstances life has dealt you. The ability to influence events, things, persons, and themselves gives people a sense of control. Psychologists Judith Rodin and Christine Timko compared residents living in a nursing home who were given some elements of control over their environment with others who were not.

Not surprisingly, those given control over aspects of their lives lived longer.[8]

The issue of control can arise, for example, if children and grandchildren decide to move a thousand miles away from the grandparents. The younger family may be excited about the move. But the grandparents may feel left behind and become depressed, as their routines and emotional attachment to the younger members of the family are challenged. Their reaction will depend on their resources for coping with the transition that they can identify using their 4 S's (situation, self, support, and strategies; see Chapter 4). Grandparents may feel very sad and deserted about "losing" an entire family. We can, however, generalize that the more you feel you can control a situation, the more likely you will be able to manage it and reduce the toll it takes on you.

We cannot avoid acknowledging that as they age, people may find themselves in situations over which they have no control. When Betty developed Lou Gehrig's disease, her adult children had to decide if a change in location would be best for her. They brought her from her hometown to a nursing home in another town to be closer to them. They moved her into a private room, but eventually found that too expensive, so they shifted her to a double room without consulting her. Betty was upset about the move. She felt out of control. It would have been helpful if they had given her the choice of rooms within the price range they could afford. It is helpful if even small choices can still be put in the hands of the person most affected.

Your Identity

Whenever you move, and wherever you move, you will think about how the transition influences the way you see yourself and the way you want others to see you. Barbara, a 68-year-old recent divorcee, knew she had to move to an apartment. She actually found one she liked in the center of the town where she was currently living, but at the last minute she realized that in a few years she would be ready for a retirement community. Barbara believed that two moves would be too disruptive, so she decided to move to the retirement community immediately. However, she kept her outside activities and decided not to be too involved with the aging part of the community designed for older residents. She chose not to take a meal plan and instead eats out or in her apartment. She wants to be identified as an active person in the community outside her residence.

Like many others, Barbara realized that her move would require her to downsize. This is a common theme that arises when we get older and relocate. Downsizing, moving to less space with fewer things, can be seen as an opportunity to be less encumbered with "stuff," as being downwardly mobile because of economic distress, or a sign of aging where you are unable to manage your "big house." One woman I interviewed said she would feel disloyal to her spouse if she were to throw things out. In the case of a retired academic I spoke with, downsizing required that he throw out some of his professional files. He sadly said, "It feels as if I am tossing out that part of my identity."

Your Attachment to Objects

Attachment theory explains our need from infancy to be connected to safe people and objects. When faced with moving or downsizing, our attachment to material objects becomes an issue. Things remind us of people, places, and activities. Giving them up is upsetting. This requires thinking through what the objects mean to you and what giving them up evokes. Some people find it useful to seek help from counselors or therapists to figure it out.

Hoarding is a adverse example of attachment to objects. At the extreme, hoarding can be a serious mental health disorder. In fact, hoarding disorder was officially recognized in the *Diagnostic and Statistical Manual of Mental Disorders, Fifth Edition*.[9] At a meeting of the Institute for Challenging Disorganization, ("the premier resource for education, research, and strategies for overcoming challenging disorganization"), a participant described the case of a woman who cluttered so extremely that her husband, wheelchair-bound, was unable to navigate from the bedroom to the kitchen.

T. M. Luhrmann, professor of anthropology at Stanford, suggested that

> locations have always been central to human thought and feeling . . . memory becomes attached to places. . . . That is also why it can be so hard to shed possessions,

because each knickknack, every book, carries the trace of a particular where and when and with whom, and we can feel that when we toss the object, part of who we are goes with it.[10]

Mary, a widow going on 6 years, is still deciding what to do about her living situation. However, she is beginning to lean toward moving close to her daughter despite the drawbacks. Living in a house that constantly needs repairs and is isolated in the winter is beginning to bother her, but she is happy she has stayed in the house with all her memories. Everyone is different, and you will need to make careful choices about which items are meaningful to you and which are just "stuff."

Location matters—this sounds like an easy concept, but the decision you make has implications that go far beyond your change in address.

Your Happiness

Does where you live affect your happiness? It depends. A Gallup Poll survey that identified the happiest and unhappiest states suggested that happiness and health go hand-in-hand. Greg Daugherty, a former retirement columnist for *Consumer Reports Money Adviser Newsletter*, wrote,

> Happiness is a combination of health and social involvement. I think it is reasonable to infer that it is best to retire to a place that offers at least one of those and ideally both . . . I also know, although only anecdotally, that many people retire to places where they find that they are unhappy and end up returning to their old areas

or somewhere in between. (personal communication, June 22, 2015)

In 2005, the World Health Organization (WHO) recognized the role of the environment in the promotion of active healthy aging for all. According to WHO,

> An age-friendly world enables people of all ages to actively participate in community activities, and treats everyone with respect, regardless of their age. It is a place that makes it easy for older people to stay connected to people that are important to them. And it helps people stay healthy and active even at the oldest ages and provides appropriate support to those who can no longer look after themselves.[11]

The Patterson Foundation, headed by visionary Debra Jacobs, has taken the lead in establishing an "age-friendly Sarasota." Jacobs reported

> that the Patterson Foundation has the opportunity to strengthen the community efforts in planning for the future livability of Sarasota County. Knowing that when we have a pulse, we have a purpose . . . people live meaningful lives, no matter what their age. There is a tremendous opportunity to learn and share knowledge that enables all generations to live well. By engaging and connecting citizens throughout Sarasota County, we are fostering wide participation in planning for a future built on aspirations and assets. (personal communication, April 22, 2016)

According to Dr. Kathy Black, lead initiative consultant for the project, the work focuses on transportation, housing, social participation, outdoor spaces and public buildings, communication and information, civic participation and employment, respect and social inclusion, and community supports and health services. Following the initiative's launch in 2015, Sarasota County residents participated in surveys and focus groups designed to assess the community's assets and aspirations within these focus areas. Nearly 1,200 residents age 50 and over responded, representing each geographic area of the county by zip code According to Dr. Black, "Sarasota is pleased to be Florida's first WHO age-friendly community."

Rodney Harrell with the AARP's Public Policy Institute developed "The Livability Index," an online tool (available at http://www.aarp.org/livabilityindex) that you can take to evaluate and compare communities on a number of categories of livability: housing, neighborhood, transportation, environment, health, engagement, and opportunity. This index will help you make wise decisions as you consider moving or remaining in a particular place.

THE MONEY ANGLE

As you have already seen in discussions of location options in this chapter, your financial resources can make a huge difference in where you live as you age. Before making any kind of decision—whether to stay in your current residence and location, or whether to move—you need to have a detailed understanding of how the decision will affect your quality of life as well as your finances.

If you live in a house or apartment that is paid off or has a very low mortgage, it could make financial sense to remain, as long as you are physically comfortable there and your income covers expenses. To know if this makes sense for you, think about future expenses as well as current ones. Will you need to hire people to help maintain the property as you get older? Do you need to make it safer for you physically, by installing a ramp, modifying door sizes, or installing grab bars? Will you have easy access to local services? If you cannot drive, will you need to pay someone to take you to shop, to medical appointments, and other tasks? Any of these factors could increase your cost of living there in the future. Increasingly, people who are committed to staying in their home are exploring new models, such as sharing with friends who help with the costs.

Some people like the idea of buying a new house or apartment to "start a new phase of life" in retirement. If you want to do this, or feel forced to by considerations such as health, family, or access to transportation, be aware that it may be difficult to get a mortgage. Since the housing bubble burst in 2008, lenders have significantly tightened their mortgage eligibility standards. Retirees who are living on a fixed or low income may find they cannot qualify because lenders often will not consider their money (e.g., in a brokerage account, in an

IRA, in an SEP) in determining eligibility. Depending on where you live, it actually may be more economical to rent a house or apartment rather than to buy one.

If you determine that you really need to relocate, you will need to price out each option not just for now but for the long-term future as well. Condo residents, for example, may be hit in the future with the costs of repairing common areas, and these special assessments can be very expensive. One condo resident, for example, is considering moving, knowing that in the next couple of years he will be required to contribute to the cost of a roof replacement. It is especially important to estimate long-term costs in the case of joining a retirement or life plan community, where you may have to make a large deposit and will encounter irrevocable fees and expenses once you make a commitment. Before you do this, ask yourself, "Once I spend a lot of my resources on a deposit, will the remaining income and savings be enough to cover my necessary expenses and provide the lifestyle I seek?"

Relocation to a different geographical area requires another level of financial planning not just for your dwelling but also for routine expenses such as utilities, food, and transportation. By searching on the Internet you can often find estimates of these costs for most locations, but the best way to pin them down is to visit and spend some time doing research on the basis of your own personal needs.

The bottom line is that you should always preface your analysis of where to live with a thorough review of your finances, current and future, before honing in on specific homes or communities.

YOUR TO-DO LIST

Given the importance of location to your happiness and your ability to age successfully, it is important to anticipate issues that might come up and figure out how to deal with them. Here are some things to think about as you decide which location is best for you.

- **Develop your criteria:** Do you want a certain type of climate? An active social life? Access to excellent health care facilities? Make a checklist and search for locations that meet your criteria. Try to visit as many sites as possible. Interview friends who have chosen various options.
- **Identify a neutral professional or professionals:** They can help you think through your options. If you have access and can afford it, this is a good time to seek advice from a financial adviser. One couple consulted their financial adviser about a possible downsizing from a large home to a retirement community. The financial planner ran the numbers to figure when they would outlive their income and the difference in cost of each scenario. They then consulted a transition company that helps individuals figure out the practical steps of any move. If money is tight, even talking through your ideas about moving with friends or family might help you make a good decision.

- **Use the transition framework to make your decision:** The transition model described in Chapter 4—identifying your resources (4 S's) for coping with change—can help. Is your situation fairly stable? Will you have enough supports in the new community or do you know where to get supports? Are you (self) flexible and able to tolerate and flourish with change? Do you use lots of strategies flexibly? Answering those questions can help you decide if this is the right time to move.

- **Do a trial run:** If you are wondering whether you should relocate when you retire or as you age, it is helpful to spend as much time as possible in the community you are considering. If feasible, it would be ideal to spend a whole year in the prospective community, but if that is not practical, visiting more than once, in different seasons, could help provide an idea of what living in the new community might be like.

- **Consult your family:** Keep in mind that your adult children have their own agendas. There are two ways to deal with this: One is to consult your family before making a decision; the other is to announce the fait accompli. I spoke with a son who does not want his widowed mother to enter a retirement community because it would eat up her money, whereas another son is thrilled that his mother will now be safe and he will not have to panic every time something goes wrong. A daughter I interviewed was dismayed that her father decided to move without consulting her.

- **Recruit a transition team to help you implement your decision:** Consult with friends who have moved, and listen to their experience and the pitfalls they encountered. You can also search for moving companies that cater to seniors who are relocating. They try to make the move as easy as possible. Some companies advertise that they will even hang your pictures and make your bed in the new home, but of course friends or family may also be willing to help you with these chores.
- **Develop a ritual to mark the move:** One couple had a party a month or so before they moved, to celebrate the wonderful years they had had in the apartment and to look to the future. They made toasts to acknowledge the past and the future.

When you face the life-changing decision of whether to move, you are the only one—in most cases, with input from family or a partner—who can ultimately come up with the right course of action. Before acting, be sure to list and evaluate all the available options. Then, to avoid too much of a shock, try to make the change gradually. For example, spend some time in the proposed new location, or rent rather than buy until you are sure. It is important for you to feel in control of the decision. Regardless of where you live, whether in independent living, cohousing, or cohabitation, make sure that there are opportunities for regular interaction with others and enjoyable activities, as well as access to health and other services you may require.

7

Cope With Health Challenges

When she was 65, Elly's vision began to deteriorate and she was diagnosed with macular degeneration. At first, only one eye was affected, so she was optimistic that she would be able to see with one good eye. She was shocked when the second eye began to deteriorate. In the past, when Elly had thought about aging, she pictured herself sitting in a rocking chair and reading. It never occurred to her that she could lose her sight. After a few months of exploring options, Elly had to face the fact that she was legally blind. For a 65-year-old woman with lots of energy, this was a shock.

After adjusting to this major change in her situation, Elly, a licensed counselor, began to take charge of her life. She initiated a counseling group for low-vision individuals at a model senior center in an urban area. It was a win-win arrangement. The members of the group were delighted about the counseling sessions, and Elly felt like she was being useful again. She investigated the technology that could help her use a computer, write emails, and search the Internet. As she helped others face incorporate new technologies into their lives, Elly began to feel more like herself. She was doing what she had always done—counsel others and work with groups.

Once Elly started to feel more like herself, she made a conscious decision to take risks. She walked everywhere and used the subway. "I used to be known as someone who runs training workshops. Now people say, 'Isn't it wonderful that she takes the metro.'" She managed to walk and take the subway to get to meetings, the theater, and dates with friends. Elly has accepted her major health setback and maintains perspective, humor, and grace, although she admits to being depressed at times. Her husband has had some health issues, and she feels terrible that she could not help as much as she would have liked. She is constantly reminded of what she cannot do.

MARSHAL ALL YOUR RESOURCES

Macular degeneration is only one of the many health shocks that can hit us as we age. Older adults can experience cancer, stroke, arthritis, diabetes, chronic obstructive pulmonary disease, amyotrophic lateral sclerosis (Lou Gehrig's disease), Parkinson's disease, obesity, depression, sexual challenges, dementia, Alzheimer's disease, and shingles, among others. Health challenges may be chronic or episodic, or they may be life-threatening or minor. In any case, a transition in health status occupies a great deal of our energy and thoughts.

The difference between an unhappy life, or one of dependency, and a fruitful and contented life in your 60s, 70s, 80s, or 90s relates not only to the nature of a health issue but also to how you assess the challenge, what you are willing to do about it, and your attitude in dealing with it. In other words, as with all of life's transitions, the key issue is whether and how you respond and take control.

Sometimes health challenges intensify because they become entangled with other personal issues, such as family or economic status. If this happens to you, try to identify all potential sources of support, such as family or community programs, not just the formal health care system. When confronted with any type of health challenge, your own or that of a family member or friend, the first thing to do is evaluate your perception of the challenge. Rate the challenge on a scale from 1 to 10, with 1 being the *least challenging* and 10 being the *most challenging*.

Next, examine your resources for coping. As discussed in Chapter 4, psychologists Richard Lazarus and Susan Folkman suggested two major approaches to coping with life's ups and downs: A problem-focused approach, which centers on changing the source of the stress, and an emotion-focused approach, which helps people manage their feelings and change their thinking.[1]

Once a health issue has been diagnosed, you can use a problem-focused approach by meeting with a medical professional and, if it seems appropriate, requesting a second medical opinion. You can also use the emotion-focused approach by looking into opportunities for counseling or therapy for yourself or others affected by the diagnosis. Try to identify community resources on health and aging that can help. A family member or a neighbor may be able to assist, for example, with transportation, with a referral to a clinic navigating Medicare or Medicaid, or with searching for solutions on the Internet. Once you have identified the resources available to you, use them.

The following case examples illustrate some of the complexities involved in coping with health challenges.

Dan

Dan, a 70-year-old man who was recently diagnosed with prostate cancer, engaged in both emotion-focused and problem-focused strategies. After reacting emotionally to the initial shock of the diagnosis, Dan focused on problem-solving. After consulting several experts to help him identify the best treatment for his particular cancer and conducting his own research, he decided to undergo radiation treatments. While he was in treatment, Dan's emotions were in an uproar. Would this cause an end to his sex life? Would he become incontinent and/or impotent? He had always seen himself as healthy and sexually active. With the support of his wife and through therapy, Dan was able to focus on his medical treatments and stay optimistic about the outcome. He felt fortunate to have many resources at his disposal—excellent doctors, money for health care costs not covered by insurance, a loving wife, and many friends. With these supports, the result of his treatment was positive and none of his worst fears materialized. After a period of recovery, he regained total continence and was able to resume his sex life.

Juanita

Juanita, a 60-year-old divorced woman with two adult sons, faces a variety of personal, health, and work challenges. She has no savings and very little income. A licensed nurse, Juanita was fired from several different jobs as a result of struggles with depression and possible bipolar disorder. She and her ex-husband tried on several occasions to reconcile, but after several traumatic events (e.g., he took money intended for her son's graduation, he had an extramarital affair), she finally opened her eyes to see what was going on in her life and vowed to do something about it. "I am ready to be happy. I pray, I am very spiritual, and my church is important to me. I want a job and a man and a home with a pool and fruit tree."

Because she was unable to get and hold a job, Juanita qualified for vocational rehabilitation. She waited a year to have a case manager assigned to her case, and during that time she spotted a notice asking for paid volunteers in a community health program at a storefront space. She was hired for the position and began receiving a small stipend ($200–$250 a month).

The program, a *healing circle*, is open to anyone in the community who needs support and help. Although it was not a religious organization, Juanita opened each support session with a prayer. She saw herself as a health educator and always offered water and fresh fruit for people who came in seeking support for a variety of health problems. In addition, she had a small suitcase of essential oils that she used to help alleviate most illnesses.

When asked if any of those who came to the store-front program had health insurance, Juanita explained that neither she nor those she served could afford insurance. Juanita handled her personal health challenges by mobilizing her resources—relying on her former in-laws, volunteering, and finding ways to live on little money. One day at church she saw a flyer about the Remote Area Medical Corps, a nonprofit organization that provides volunteer free dental, vision, and medical care, as well as preventive services and health education. Attending one of their free clinics, Juanita received an eye exam, two pairs of glasses, and a Pap smear.

The healing circle where Juanita works is located in a low-income section of a city with a population of 50,000 people. The physician on staff devotes her time and energy to making health care available for this community. The programs are designed to encourage participants to become health learners and health advocates. These sessions are peer-led self-management groups that emphasize stress management. Participants are taught to (a) apply skills that reduce emergency room visits, (b) identify options so that they can manage their illnesses more effectively, and (c) learn to manage the intense emotions surrounding their health transitions. Each session focuses on a different health challenge. For example, at one of the healing circle sessions, the majority of people present were survivors or family members of cancer patients.

This concept, more often called *talking circles*, originated in Native American communities and has evolved into use for communities dealing with issues such as addiction and alcoholism. The National Resource Center for Native American Aging and the Administration on Aging, for example, have used talking circles to promote diabetes education and health in tribal areas. Community centers for the elderly and hospice are two other areas that use talking circles.[2]

YOUR COGNITIVE HEALTH

Joan noticed strange behavior in her normally calm husband, Greg. He was forgetting things more frequently, and she became alarmed. They started to cope with this issue by setting up appointments with a well-known neurologist, and after a number of tests, it was determined that Greg had mild cognitive impairment (MCI), an intermediate stage between the expected cognitive decline of normal aging and the more serious decline of dementia. MCI can involve problems with memory, language, thinking, and judgment that are greater than normal age-related changes; a person experiencing MCI, as well as friends and family, may be aware that memory or mental function has "slipped," but generally the changes are not severe enough to interfere with day-to-day activities. MCI, however, may increase the risk of later progressing to dementia, Alzheimer's disease, or other medical or neurological conditions. Often partners, spouses, or adult children overreact to this kind of diagnosis and request that an individual with MCI be put on drugs. However, in Joan's case, she followed the advice of the neurologist, who referred Greg to a group that works with individuals with cognitive issues by helping them make lifestyle choices to preserve and improve their "brain reserve," defined as the brain's resilience, which can be protected by making lifestyle choices that include changing diet and developing or increasing exercise. Families, as well as participants, receive support through weekly and monthly meetings. Joan and Greg decided to continue with this program and plan to have another full evaluation in 6 months.

A wide range of conditions and severity can affect cognitive health. But there is no doubt that as our lifespan increases, so does the number of people who experience dementia and Alzheimer's disease, which is complex and challenging and for which there is no cure. These conditions affect those who experiences them and also the people around them.

In 2007, Ralph, age 62, noticed that his wife, Sarah, was experiencing memory loss. He admitted that, like many others in his situation, he went into denial. After all, he said, "Everyone loses keys [or] forgets names, so it is no big deal." He thought Sarah was depressed and she went to a psychiatrist who then sent her to a neurologist. A year later, Sarah was diagnosed with MCI, but that diagnosis later changed to frontal temporal dementia, which, according to the Alzheimer's Association, is a disease in which "nerve cell damage . . . leads to loss of function in [certain] brain regions, which variably cause deterioration in behavior and personality, language disturbances, or alterations in muscle or motor function."[3]

Several years after her diagnosis, Sarah's behavior changed. She resisted taking her pills and started expressing anger toward Ralph. The effects of her disease have led to major changes in their lives. He realized they needed to simplify their lives; he retired, they sold their home, and they moved into a community for older people where meals and help were available.

Based on his own difficult journey, Ralph shared what he had learned with others: Do not ignore signs of trouble, view the situation honestly, seek professional help as early as possible, and start lifestyle changes immediately. Ralph commented, "I want to make my wife happy." A doctor explained that Ralph's job was to keep Sarah safe and happy as long as possible and when she was angry or agitated, he needed to realize it is not his fault.

Because so many health problems, including cognitive decline, can be ameliorated, if not "cured," by making lifestyle changes, these changes should be started as soon as the problem is acknowledged. Most of the programs that address lifestyle changes include changes to diet, exercise, meditation and mindfulness, and, maybe most important, social engagement.

YOUR HEALTH AND YOUR HAPPINESS

During one of my conversation groups, one woman explained that as people were exchanging best wishes at a holiday party, she told everyone, "It will be happy if we are healthy. Good health leads to happiness." Many scientific studies are finding a connection between psychological and physical well-being. More specifically, some of these suggest that how happy you are may make a difference in your cardiovascular health and your propensity to become disabled.

A review of more than 200 studies by Julia Boehm, Loryana Vie, and Laura Kubzansky found a connection between positive psychological attributes, such as happiness, optimism, and life satisfaction, and a lowered risk of cardiovascular disease.[4] They cautioned against interpreting their results as meaning that if you are happy, you will prevent heart attacks. Their point was that if you have a good sense of well-being, it is easier to maintain good habits: exercising, eating a balanced diet, and getting enough sleep. People who have an optimistic mind-set may be more likely to engage in healthy behaviors because they perceive them as helpful in achieving their goals. Being able to manage emotional ups and downs is important for the health of body and mind. Laura Kubzansky, professor at the Harvard School of Public Health, conducted research on happiness:

> In a 2007 study that followed more than 6,000 men and women age 25 to 74 for 20 years, emotional vitality— a sense of enthusiasm, hopefulness, engagement in life, and the ability to face life's stresses with emotional balance—appeared to reduce the risk of coronary heart disease. The protective effect was distinct and measurable, even when taking into account such wholesome behaviors as not smoking and regular exercise.[5]

For now, these studies can only show associations; they do not provide hard evidence of cause and effect. But some researchers speculated that positive mental states do have a direct effect on the body, perhaps by reducing damaging physical processes.

How can we develop the kinds of behaviors necessary for a healthy life? One answer may be to practice mindfulness. Ellen Langer, author of *Counter Clockwise: Mindful Health and the Power of Possibility*, described mindfulness as the process of "actively noticing things. . . . It is the way we feel when we are fully engaged."[6] Although many use mindfulness to refer to meditation, Langer pointed out that mindfulness and meditation are not the same. According to the *Merriam-Webster* dictionary, *mindfulness* is "the quality or state of being mindful; the practice of maintaining a nonjudgmental state of heightened or complete awareness of one's thoughts, emotions, or experiences on a moment-to-moment basis." The same source defines *meditation* as "the act or process of spending time in quiet thought."[7]

Being mindful prompts us to notice our bodies, reinforcing the notion of interconnections between mind and body. That led Langer (and many others) to conclude that it is possible to take control of your health.

Langer designed the counterclockwise study to see if experiencing yourself as you were when you were younger could change your behavior. The study group retrofitted an old hotel to look as it did in 1957. They then identified men in their 70s to go to the hotel and live as if they were in the 1950s—with music and magazines from that period. Immersed in the past, some of the men who were using canes had stopped using them by the time the study was over. This revolutionary study opened the floodgates to additional research that bolstered the theory that your mind can influence your health and behavior. As a result of this study, Langer articulated her vision of psychology: "In the psychology of possibility, we search for the answer to how to improve, not merely to adjust."[8]

TAKE CONTROL

As we age, many of us need to answer the question, how can we lead a full life even if our routines are disrupted by health problems? Consider some of the examples of health challenges we may face as we age. One woman, part of a walking group, found that her knees were hurting so much during the walks that she came home exhausted. She considered giving up her participation in the group. Another woman described her husband's depression after being told he should stop riding his bicycle. Her husband was a world-class rider, but he had recently been diagnosed with prostate cancer. His reaction to the advice he should stop riding his bicycle was, "Is it worth living if I cannot ride?" An award-winning architect bought tools and started building sculptures and fixing things around his home when he retired. But over time, his arthritis became so acute that he could no longer use his hands or his tools. He gave the tools to Habitat for Humanity and is very pessimistic about his future.

In situations such as these, Langer suggested that we look at our health in a mindful way, that we view it as a continuum rather than an either–or option. The woman with problem knees could consider several possibilities—exploring ways to strengthen her knees, receiving occasional cortisone shots, or walking part way with her companions and then sitting and waiting for the group to return. The man who can no longer ride his bike for hours at a time might be able to modify his goals and his routine so that he could still ride without injuring himself. The architect could offer pro bono consulting services to Habitat for Humanity, in addition to giving them his tools—or offer his services to other nonprofit organizations or young architects starting their careers. He could even teach a class on architectural monuments or styles in a "lifelong learning" program at a local college.

In other words, do not assume you have to give up cherished activities entirely—you can never have sex, you can never walk with the group, you can never ride your bike, or you have to give up your professional identity. Make your mind a partner in maintaining your health. Sometimes all that is needed is to take the time to analyze your situation and brainstorm ways to achieve your goals.

There is some evidence that as people age, they feel less in control of their lives. Ellen Langer and Judith Rodin showed that

> when we examined age differences . . . we found a lower sense of control for those in later life. . . . Almost 80% of the young said they are in control, whereas it was 71% for the middle-age, and only 62% for older adults. These age differences are not because of group variations in education, income, or health.[8]

Suggesting the potential benefits of taking conscious steps toward control, Margie Lachman reported on a group of older adults who reversed memory loss and eliminated falls after participating in a training program designed to help people believe they could age more successfully.[9]

Investigate whether your community offers support groups or programs that address your own situation. One example is the Aging Mastery Program (AMP) developed by the National Council on Aging. It is a comprehensive and fun approach to aging well that encourages taking actions to enhance your health, financial well-being, social connectedness, and overall quality of life. Central to the AMP philosophy is the belief that modest lifestyle changes can produce big results and that people can be empowered and supported to cultivate health and longevity. Equally important, the program encourages mastery and developing sustainable behaviors over time. Participants go through a 10-week core program followed by optional elective classes and activities. At the moment, the program is in place in over 121 sites throughout the United States. The program evaluators have reported an increase in healthy behaviors for participants, including better eating and exercise habits, improved communication with health care providers, and improved self-administration of medications. On the National Council of Aging website (https://www.ncoa.org/healthy-aging/aging-mastery-program/) you can search for AMP programs and other programs, such as senior centers and fall prevention programs, that might be helpful.

THE MONEY ANGLE

Despite the existence of Medicare and Medicaid, for many in our society, access to health care depends on their ability to find funding and support outside these systems. Medical care and insurance premiums usually account for a big chunk of the household budget as we age—one that tends to increase as we get older. A study by the Employee Benefit Research Institute found that people age 65 to 74 spent $4,383 out-of-pocket on health care, while those 85 and older spent $6,603, approximately 19% of their household expenses.[10]

Prescription drugs have become an increasingly important component of health care expenses. One decision you must face is whether to pay the premiums for Medicare Part D, which ultimately reduces the price of prescriptions if you spend a certain amount of money on them. It is a risk, but on the other hand, if you are very healthy, you may decide to save the cost of that premium. When you need a prescription, always ask your doctor if a generic drug, rather than one with a brand name, is equally effective, and/or if the doctor or the pharmacy knows of a discount plan that will reduce your cost. You can personally research the possibility of discounts by looking up the relevant pharmaceutical company on the Internet.

A serious health care money crunch may hit in different ways—in the event of a disability or a chronic or catastrophic illness. For some people, the hospital, doctor, prescription, and caregiving costs associated with a health crisis create a domino effect that makes it difficult or impossible to keep up with the rent or other household expenses. Because it is usually impossible to predict the state of your health throughout your entire life, it is crucial to take some steps to protect yourself and others in your family from a health-related financial crisis that could occur as you get older.

Do not dismiss the potential for positive effects from adopting routines to keep your mind and body healthy. Physical exercise, to the extent your doctor says it is safe, should be a priority, as should eating a healthy diet. And do not forget to exercise your mind as well: Although much more research must be done, it is clear that even simple activities, such as doing the daily crossword or reading the newspaper, can help keep you sharp and deter the onset of diseases, such as dementia.

YOUR TO-DO LIST

There are many strategies available as you take positive steps toward a healthy life.

- **Financial strategies:** First, inform yourself about your current and potential future health insurance coverage. What is covered and what is not? If you are not retired yet, find out if your work health insurance will cover you after you retire. If so, will you be able to maintain it and at what cost? Will it cover your spouse or partner? If you are under 65, do not have employer insurance, and are ineligible for Medicare, do you meet the need requirements to receive Medicaid, or will you need to buy insurance on the open market? This is basic information you should, ideally, learn before you retire. You can call your local Social Security office to request an appointment to get an explanation of these programs. Second, explore whether to purchase long-term care insurance. For those who can afford the premiums—especially single persons who may not be able to call on close relatives or friends in a care crisis—this could be helpful. If you are thinking about buying, be sure to compare policies, including whether they support in-home care or out-of-home care, to make sure you get the best services for the least cost.

- **Legal strategies:** Avoid confusion and anxiety about health care decisions for yourself and those close to you. Secure a living will and a health care power of attorney to spell out your wishes in the event that you become incapable of making decisions regarding your care, and appoint a person to make decisions on your behalf. Once you have the documents, share them with your family or others close to you who need to know about them.

- **Use professionals to help you:** It is critical to have a lawyer and financial planner you trust. You need to get all your legal documents in order, including your living will and a form identifying your health care surrogates. Doing this when you are well will eliminate potential conflicts after you become ill or die. To find professionals that you can afford, investigate legal aid, the Salvation Army, and other nonprofit community resources. It takes time and energy to find the right place to get help.

- **Read books for advice on a number of health subjects:** Many older people worry about their sexual health, for example. Author Michael Castleman, who writes frequently on the topic, suggests ways for couples to express affection, love, and eroticism without intercourse.[11]

148

Aging can bring a wide variety of health transitions. And your health situation is related to your finances and location. What can you afford? Where will you live? Will you have long-term care? There are many decisions to make.

As human beings growing older in the 21st century, we are experiencing a time of great changes: Scientific strides, and increasing longevity, have brought health transitions that many of our predecessors did not have to address. Yet, as Lachman pointed out in reporting her research, the basic strategies recommended for a long and healthy life have not changed all that much over the last 2,000 years. They are strategies

> to adopt a regimen of health; to practice moderate exercise; and to take just enough food and drink to restore our strength and not to overburden it. Nor, indeed are we to give our attention solely to the body; much greater care is due to the mind and soul; for they, too, like lamps grow dim with time, unless we keep them supplied with oil. (Cicero, trans. 1946, XI. 36)[9]

Sometimes ancient wisdom is the best. The previous quote is from the Roman philosopher, politician, and orator Marcus Tullius Cicero when he was 62 years old. Now, as then, the basic paths to health are clear. Two thousand years later, we still need to follow those paths, and if we encounter challenges that make us deviate, we must do our best to return to them by strengthening our personal coping strategies.

8

Understand Your Family Transitions

At an informal evening gathering with several couples, talk inevitably centered on family. Surprisingly, it got quite personal. One woman, an accomplished lawyer, shared that she had been feeling jealous of her grown child. She said she felt pangs of jealousy every so often now that her husband, also a lawyer, would ask their 45-year-old daughter for advice instead of his wife.

In response, a man mentioned that he had been caring for his aging mother on a daily basis. His brother lived in another country and called only occasionally. The mother would brag to her friends about her distant son who called, but not about the son who helped her every single day.

A couple mentioned their depression in regard to their son's divorce. They no longer had access to their grandchildren on a regular basis and could not understand why the couple pulled apart. A growing number of divorces occur after age 50, with more than 25% of divorces including couples who are 50 or older. This has led some to refer to this transition as *gray divorces*.[1]

Anger, jealousy, love, hate, worry, happiness, and sadness are all part of family life; they do not disappear because we are older. Complicated family situations today are a sharp contrast to *Leave It to Beaver*, a situation comedy that ran from 1957 to 1963, which portrayed a nuclear family of four, living in suburbia. During the show's heyday, it was often viewed as a template for the American family. In the 14th edition of *Family in Transition*, Arlene and Jerome Skolnick chronicled the evolution of the American family from the *Beaver* model to a set of much more varied models that include an acceptance of cohabitation, same-sex relationships, and women working outside the home, among others.[2] The template for the 21st century family is, in many cases, very different from the one in the days of *Leave It to Beaver*: We have two-parent families, one-parent families, adopted families, same-sex families, multiracial families, stepfamilies, and unmarried couples of all ages who consider themselves families.

Although the "traditional" family is in decline, many new forms have replaced it. The trends these changes describe influence our lives and our lifestyle options as we age, presenting new challenges to our generation and those that follow. Some trends that especially have had an impact on older people include the following:

- **People are becoming part of four-generation families:** Three- and four-generation families are becoming more common. According to a Pew

Research Center report, multigeneration households have increased substantially between 1980 and 2012.[3]

- **People meet on the Internet:** Ron, a 90-year-old grandfather of nine children and great-grandfather of six, was married for 60 years. He became his wife's hands-on caregiver for the last 5 years of her life. After he became a widower, his daughter enrolled him in an Internet dating site, where he met an 85-year-old woman with whom he now lives. His experience, at an advanced age, of seeking a new partner on the Internet—and actually finding one to live with—is increasingly common.

- **People are promoting decades of shared lives with other generations:** There is good news and bad news with this trend. The good news is that we can see our grandchildren marry and enjoy watching members of our extended family set out on different life paths. The bad news is that by living longer we may also see our children die and suffer with them, run out of money, need help, and be forced into raising our grandchildren instead of enjoying the carefree retirement about which we had dreamt. Sometimes, for better or for worse, this means living in the same house with an adult child.

- **People are becoming members of the *sandwich generation*:** Forty million Americans have a parent age 65 or older and are simultaneously raising a young child or are financially supporting a grown child.[4] Juggling one's own life priorities while attending to those of two other generations is more likely to be stressful than rewarding. Gunhild Hagestad studied the different ways the middle generation influences and interacts with parents and children. For example, middle-aged parents helped the older generation with practical matters such as finding the right health care plan, at the same time they were encouraging their children to get on with their adult lives. The sandwich generation tries to influence both generations to take care of health issues.

The more we delve into the nuances of family relationships, the more we realize that the permutations are almost endless and that an individual's personal family scenario is very likely to change over time. But there is no question that certain shifts in relationships have become a common feature of American family life. As these relationships change, the result is not necessarily better or worse. The challenge is to bend them in a positive direction.

There are so many aspects of family life that it was necessary to narrow the list down to four common examples of how relationships change as we get older: Parents finding that their adult children try to "boss them around;" grandparents raising grandchildren; spouses becoming caregivers; and breakups in the family, including couples who divorce. Of course, these are not the only family transitions that will occur, but they are examples of how life changes.

PARENTS AND CHILDREN: THE BALANCE SHIFTS

When you are a child, your parents are in charge, often hovering over you to ensure that you are clean, fed, and happy. Over time, the balance begins to shift until parent and child are coequal and independent adults. Then as parents age, adult children begin to take a stronger role in managing their parents' lives. Many parents, regardless of cultural or socioeconomic states, seem to rebel against what they see as a loss of their own independence.

After Ana's husband died, she had shoulder replacement surgery. Her daughter was very solicitous during the entire period of the operation and recuperation, but when Ana recovered and was back at her exercise class, as well as volunteering at a nonprofit, her daughter hovered over her constantly, calling her with questions. "Have you called the doctor?" "Do you think you are forgetting appointments?" Ana realized her daughter was still trying to help, but Ana felt as if her daughter was trying to boss and control Ana's life. They had a talk and Ana tried to make it clear she was still in charge of her life.

Similar stories were told at a lunch get-together sponsored by a senior center located in a low-income neighborhood. The 25 women in attendance expressed distress that their adult children or even siblings boss them around. Although the women have physical challenges, they are determined to maintain their independence. One woman exclaimed, "Why doesn't my son trust me to call if I need help?" Listening to these women reminded me of meeting with the middle-class book club members who also complained about adult children trying to "control" their lives.

In a very moving novel by Kent Haruf, *Our Souls at Night*, two lonely, older people got together each night, held each other, and talked intimately.[5] Soon the woman's son put a stop to it. He refused to let her keep in touch with his son, her grandson, if she kept this relationship going. This is an extreme example of one generation trying to control the other.

Psychologists talk about asymmetry of investment—originally, parents invest more in children when children are young and then, as one person put it, "the womb turns" and adult children start to lead the way.

POSSIBILITIES, NOT PROBLEMS

Much of the literature on intergenerational relationships focuses on the negative impact of these shifts in family connections. However, there is another possibility: promoting adult children and their parents as colleagues. Roxanne, a co-owner of a boutique PR firm, hired her mother to be her "Woman Friday." This became a win-win situation. Her mother, who had been helping out with the refreshments and arrangements for a photo shoot, explained, "Working for my daughter has added 10 years to my life. I love it. I have a place to go, a purpose, and added zest to my life." Sean, a client developer for a major marketing company, lives in a tree house on his mother's property in Oregon. He hired his mother to help him with public relations and depends on her to edit all of his writing. Daniel, a computer consultant, took charge when his father retired from his carpet cleaning business. Daniel convinced his father to learn about computers. Now they make every house call together. Daniel's father handles the books, makes the appointments, and once again feels useful.

Even if the adult child and parent are not working together, an adult child might just be the one to stimulate retired parents to revitalize their lives by igniting new or previous interests or activities. After Hugo sold his drugstore, he was depressed, bored, and spent all day watching TV. His son remembered his father's love of baseball and literally dragged him to a senior baseball league. This was the beginning of Hugo's reengaging in life. He ended up playing in the senior baseball league, made new friends, and started going out for a beer with some of them.

GRANDPARENTS RAISING GRANDCHILDREN

Seven percent of children under 18—nearly 5 million—live in grandparent-headed households, a number that is on the rise. Two thirds of these grandparents raising children are under 60, 51% are Caucasian, 29% are African American, and 19% are Hispanic. In other words, this phenomenon has emerged in many parts of our society.[6]

Raising a grandchild can offer rewards to the grandparent—a chance to develop a close relationship with the child and see his or her progress through life. But this situation can also generate a lot of stress.

As a surrogate parent, the grandparent is "off-time," playing a role that is usually unexpected and often unwanted. Instead of a warm "love then leave" visit to see little grandchildren, the grandparent now is on 24/7 duty. Life routines must change, relationships with friends are put on hold, and assumptions about how their world works are in flux.[7]

The University of Maryland housed a major project on grandparents raising grandchildren. We conducted focus groups with grandparents about their role, worked with the school system to help liaison between school and family, and lobbied for legislation to support grandparents. We also worked with Howard University to train a corps of grandparents who then went into the community to support other grandparents in their struggles. Each trained grandparent received a business card and a small budget for emergencies. They became paraprofessionals and links to the community.

Some typical examples from the University of Maryland study include the following. A 74-year-old grandmother had been taking care of 7-year-old Robbie most of his life because his mother had died of AIDS; 45-year-old Bertha had taken in 10-year-old Maria, whose mother had schizophrenia. Maria was a latchkey child, but the key was to grandma's house, not her mother's. Furthermore, a large percentage of the children, parents, and grandparents caught in this web are affected by a disability. It is estimated that 125,000 children will lose their mothers to AIDS, emotional problems, drug and/or alcohol addictions, and poor health. In other words, this is clearly a situation where one generation's disability becomes another generation's liability.

We asked the grandparents we interviewed (most of whom were at the poverty level) to describe the strains they felt. A retired postal employee had looked forward to freedom during her retirement, but she spoke for most of the other grandparents we interviewed when she expressed her heartfelt view that she would not have it otherwise. She loved her grandchildren, and putting her life on hold was a minor consideration if it meant giving them a chance.

The grandparent paraprofessionals were great resources and advocates for other grandparents raising grandchildren. For example, when a grandparent did not know what to do when she was not the legal guardian (many of the grandparents would not testify against their children, always hoping that the parents' lives would turn around), the paraprofessional could arrange a meeting with a legal aid attorney or uncover needed resources.

SPOUSES AS CAREGIVERS

Dr. Karen Hutchins Pirnot, a psychologist, wrote *Nothing Left to Burn*, the story of her unrelenting role as her husband's wife, caregiver, caretaker, occasional enemy, and constant advocate in the health care system.[8] In the book, she shares the story of her journey as her husband, Charlie, succumbs to Alzheimer's disease. In reality, the book chronicles two journeys: Charlie's, as his memory deteriorates and his frustration increases, and Karen's, as she moves from acting as a collaborative caregiver to realizing she has lost him and fearing she will lose herself.

Karen's experience demonstrates one aspect of "the new normal" we face as we age and, especially, as we live longer than previous generations. As a psychologist and writer, as well as a caregiver, she helps bring into focus the challenges that aging brings to family relationships.

In an interview, Karen shared that caregiving had become especially complicated by the revelation that her husband had invested their savings in a financial scam, and that when he became too difficult to care for at home, she would need to rely on Medicaid support to place him in a facility. She described meeting with an eldercare lawyer to help her identify options, as she searched for a residential situation that met her standards and her financial ability. In her book, she described her loneliness as a caregiver, trying to anticipate her husband's needs and prevent him from injuring himself or something in the house. She found the anticipation exhausting. Often, she said, "I went to bed tired and I got up feeling I had not slept at all."[8]

What kept her going was writing—she finished her first book and is now working on a new book describing "a positive reinforcement program I have been using with Charlie" for 9 years—an approach she believes has helped maintain "cooperation and trust" with her husband as his disease progressed.

Her story is far from unique. An estimated 44 million adults in the United States are providing personal assistance for family members with disabilities or other care needs. Thirty-four million adults provide care to someone 50 years or older, and 22 million are caring for someone 75 or older. One in 10 caregivers, most of them elderly themselves, are providing assistance to a spouse.[9]

At best, caregiving is a stressful, emotionally draining activity, and this is true regardless of the relationship of the caregiver to the recipient of care. Caregivers almost always must subordinate their personal priorities to the health care needs of another person. But when that person has been your life partner, it can be especially challenging to manage the relationship, which inevitably undergoes major changes.

In addition to the practical demands of caregiving, members of the LGBTQ community may also be wrestling with issues such as access to a life partner who is hospitalized or in a nursing home; legal authority to make medical decisions for that person; and financial struggles because of policies in areas, such as pensions, health insurance (including Medicaid), and Social Security, that do not treat them as a spouse.

Although the numbers have not been pinned down, an increasing number of people in the LGBTQ community are caregivers, who may not be married but are committed to a life partner or who depend on a network of informal caregivers. According to SAGE and the Movement Advancement Project,

> While LGBT older adults are only half as likely as heterosexual older adults to have close relatives to call for help, they are more likely than the larger population to rely on families of choice. [However,] while nontraditional caregivers are an important asset, relying exclusively on such caregivers presents tremendous challenges . . . because they are not recognized as legitimate (and/or preferred) providers of care by civil and social institutions and the law.[10]

Various Coping Methods

To understand the issues faced by a range of caregivers more fully, I met with a group of six women and two men who are providing care to their spouses. *Relentless* is the word that best reflects how these caregivers describe their lot. Most of them expressed deep love for their spouses, but at the same time they noted the losses brought about by their situation. "The woman I am living with now is not the woman I married," one man said. Others talked about the loss of their companions and their "shrinking social life and loss of friends." One woman said about her husband, "I used to be so happy. Now I am not happy anymore." Another woman expressed resentment about "not having conversations like we used to have."

Another woman echoed these sentiments when she said,

> I keep wondering: "Will I ever have fun again?" This period of my life reminds me of when we had small

children. I was never totally relaxed. Now it is about my husband. I now take care of the mechanics of living—banking, tickets, packing, watching his every move, walking him to the bathroom [and] worrying, worrying, worrying about money, especially if I were to die first.

Many wonder how long this situation will go on. One man explained, "We have been married for over 40 years, we did everything together, we were true partners, and now she gets lost in the house where we have lived for 15 years." Members of the group knew they must take care of themselves, but they found it difficult with the demands they face. Several members said they had to retire early because balancing caregiving and a job was overwhelming. One man is getting to the end of his rope. Despite the physical assistance he provides his wife, she does not appreciate him: "The love and appreciation are gone. That is hard to live with."

The previously described case of Karen and Charlie can serve as an example for analyzing how to cope with caregiving and the other strains that evolve from difficult family relationships. The critical question for Karen is how she can meet her own needs and keep her own identity while she is caring and arranging care for her Charlie. When she became a caregiver, Karen's life totally changed. She went from being a professional therapist and writer to being totally focused on meeting her husband's needs. Her relationship with her husband changed from being an equal partner to being in charge of a dependent person. Her day-to-day life was totally turned around from being someone on the move to staying home with Charlie full time. And, probably most important, she changed the way she saw herself. Formerly, she felt in charge, on top of their retirement years. Now she is trying to figure out how to manage her new responsibilities, how to arrange care for Charlie, and how to maintain her sanity. In other words, her transition—like that of many caregivers—has been major. Her *roles, relationships, routines,* and *assumptions* have changed. How can she cope?

There are no easy answers, but here are a few guidelines that might help Karen and others who are contending with stress in family relationships.

- **Remember, today is not forever:** Try to take one day at a time realizing that, as time goes by, solutions will present themselves and there will eventually be a resolution.

- **Set boundaries:** One man with Parkinson's disease asked his wife who was going on a business trip, "Why are you leaving me?" She explained that they could use the money and that caregivers need time off. He agreed: "You are right. Have a wonderful time."

- **Explore resources in the community:** As long as we do not need them, we may not be aware of community resources, so we need to search them out. One resource that has helped many families whose loved one cannot live alone safely are adult day centers. These centers provide a safe environment where the person in need of care can have fun, enjoy companionship, and participate in programs and activities while family members and caregivers have time to care for themselves. A good way to start researching this option is through the Internet. Another resource could be asking friends to help.

- **Use multiple coping strategies:** One member of the caregiving group I interviewed reported, "The group is my sanity. I look at this group as if it is an AA meeting." One member goes to a therapist, several keep journals, and another goes to the theatre as often as she can get respite care. One couple cries together, others talk with their children.

A Widow-in-Waiting: My Story

I empathize with the caregivers I interviewed, because I too have been a caregiver for my spouse. When I was in my late 70s, I went through a crisis I called "being a widow-in-waiting." One day, I was called to the emergency room of a Washington, DC, hospital because my husband, Steve, had tumbled down the 188-foot subway escalator at Dupont Circle. It was a miracle that he had survived. Steve had healed, but he was never the same after the accident. First he required a cane, then a walker, and finally a wheelchair. Then came a pacemaker, a hip and knee replacement, a heart bypass, and other minor surgeries.

During this 6-year stretch—and especially once Steve entered hospice care—I began to see myself as a widow-in-waiting. Everything revolved around his health and his care. My life was an endless succession of cancellations, contradictions, conflict, and coping. For a long time, I even put off surgery I needed because I did not want to be immobilized or away from Steve. During those years, Steve was frail; he developed dementia, and his quality of life was diminished. I wanted him to live, but I prayed for him to die. I wanted to be with him all the time, yet I also wanted to be out doing things. I wanted time to stand still, but I wanted time to move forward so I could start living into my own future as opposed to being in an endless holding pattern.

How I Coped

At first, my coping was dysfunctional. I had two car accidents. One occurred when I was rushing home to assist Steve and drove into the bus station. I was required to attend traffic school and pay an enormous fee, and I saw my insurance premium raised. The good news was that I had not hurt anyone—just my car. This accident alerted me to the fact that I was not coping well.

What helped me get through this period was friends and family, particularly our adult children, their spouses, and our grandchildren. They visited, they called, and they cared. It also helped to talk with other widows-in-waiting and read books on the subject—Gail Sheehy's *Passages in Caregiving: Turning Chaos Into Confidence* felt like my story.[11]

How I Moved On

When Steve died, I was actually in a rehab center following emergency back surgery and a hip replacement. My son and daughter-in-law stayed with Steve every minute during his last days, and our daughter visited as often as she could, comforting us both. Strangely, my being ill was a blessing. I was in a cocoon for 4 months. Sociologist Gunhild Hagestad described her own illness as a period when she was "out of time," a period she was no longer connected to the daily routines of life.[12] Being out of time provided a protected period for me to grieve. I moved back into time gradually—first with care at home, then with lots of physical therapy and a determination to walk again.

Five months after Steve's death, with my recovery well underway, I arranged a memorial for him in Washington, DC—a celebration of Steve's life and his contributions to the labor movement. I felt that this ritual was important in enabling me and others in the family to move ahead into a new phase of life.

By then I was no longer a widow-in-waiting, a distraught widow, or a patient with medical problems. I was becoming the same optimistic person I had always been, but I was now carving out a new life strengthened by almost 50 years in a marriage filled with love, romance, fun, and excitement. I was ready to move on.

RESOLVE BROKEN RELATIONSHIPS

A 60-year-old man resented how his parents had treated him when he was a child, and he was tempted to not go to his father's funeral. He also described how his two sisters no longer talked to each other. A 65-year-old woman has not talked to her daughter in years, largely because of a strained relationship with her son-in-law. We all know of cases of divorce, which affects all generations involved.

Once a relationship is broken, we enter into a period of reevaluation, and finally make a decision about whether to try to repair the relationship or just walk away and stay away. The big question is what, if anything, you should do about a ruptured or broken relationship. As you decide on a possible course of action, here are some strategies to consider.

Take Time to Grieve

Broken relationships are transitions—the more invested you are in the relationship, the more difficult the transition. These relationships evoke complicated reactions. You are dealing with an event—the breakup of a relationship. You are also dealing with many nonevents—what you had expected is not occurring. For example, a mother and daughter have stopped talking. That is a major event, but they are also dealing with nonevents, such as celebrations, family occasions, and memories that are not being shared. Because this situation has been going on for a long time, it might help the mother to join a grief group or talk to a grief counselor as a first step toward mending the relationship.

Develop a Leave-Taking Ritual

We have all dealt with the ending of a relationship that was important to us. Confusion and ambivalence precede the actual decision to stay or not to stay. Sara Lawrence-Lightfoot pointed out the importance of handling exits well, which should include leave-taking rituals. In her book, *Exit: The Endings That Set Us Free.* She used the example of the Peace Corps to show the need for attention to be paid to leave taking.[13] Much time was spent orienting new recruits, but much less time was spent helping volunteers adjust to returning to their own societies. Similarly, a great deal of time may be spent on planning a wedding, but if the marriage ends, less time is spent on figuring out a way to exit responsibly. Some leave-taking rituals include journal writing—taking time each day to write down your emotional reactions—and making a time and place to meditate.

Learn About Collaborative Divorce

Collaborative divorce, which is gaining traction, was developed to help people work out a harmonious way to end a marriage outside the court system, while keeping lines of communication open. The article "Collaborative

Divorce: A Win-Win Approach" describes the process.[14] Rather than two lawyers, a couple hires a team—a lawyer, an accountant, and a financial planner. Together with their team, they look at the entire picture with the goal of resolving the conflict peacefully.

Consider Forgiveness

"Why should I forgive?" asked Cora, a member of one of my conversation groups. "After all, what he did was unforgiveable." Forgiveness is not about the perpetrator of harm. It is about you. It is about freeing yourself from hatred, from angry feelings, and from being hurt. Robert D. Enright offered a process to help the forgiver in his book *Forgiveness Is a Choice: A Step-by-Step Process for Resolving Anger and Restoring Hope.* Enright pointed out that forgiveness does not deny that we have been hurt. We have a right to feel hurt, angry, or resentful. Forgiveness is not condoning, excusing, forgetting, or justifying.[15]

The following is an example of forgiving and forgetting. A young woman, Wanda, described her adolescence as a time when she hated to bring friends home in case her mother was drunk. Her mother embarrassed her and made her feel ashamed. She remembered one night when her mother chased her around the kitchen with a knife. Years later, Wanda expressed how grateful she was for her experience. If her mother had been less volatile, she might have stayed in her hometown. Instead, she moved away and developed her own identity.

When her mother became very ill and had to stop drinking, Wanda began to understand the cause of her mother's alcoholism and to forgive her. Now Wanda is free and remembers her mother with love and appreciation for all the things she did—ice skating together in the park, joint art lessons, and shopping for fun clothes. Over time, Wanda was able to see the total picture and put the negatives in perspective. Forgiveness can be freeing; it is the beginning of something new.

Explore Reconciliation

It is certainly possible to forgive without reconciliation, but you realize that one of the options in repairing a broken relationship is to get back together and negotiate a new phase in the relationship. Reconciliation is often difficult to achieve because most relationships have patterns, habits, and comfort zones. Clearly, if the relationship is to work, reconciliation will have to force the creation of new patterns, habits, and comfort zones. It is a new relationship with an old connection.

THE MONEY ANGLE

Almost every family faces a money issue at some point. When you are younger and working, the discussions revolve around who makes how much money, creating spending priorities, and who gets to make those decisions. As you age, many basic issues remain, but they may be complicated by factors such as late-life marriages, divorce, health status, and limited resources.

Consider some examples. One big issue is who controls the money in the household. A change in physical or mental health status may require a change in a long-term money routine. If your husband has always controlled the checkbook and is now making unnecessary purchases from shopping channels and investing in penny stocks sold over the telephone, how can you stop these behaviors? If the electric company calls to say you have not paid your bill and you find several months' worth of bills in your desk drawer, can you admit that you might need help managing your money?

Getting older also raises the difficult issue of analyzing how long our money will last. When you retire, should you treat yourself to an around-the-world trip, or should you save money for an uncertain future? Should you hang on to your savings or invest them in a retirement or senior care community, even if you do not plan to live in the community now and even if it may turn out that you are perfectly able to remain in your own home for the long run?

How you plan and manage your finances can also prompt tricky questions about inheritances. Should you plan to enjoy life to the fullest and die poor, or should you save up to leave money to your children and grandchildren? One common issue is how to divide assets among children. Should the child who is a caregiver for a parent receive more of an inheritance than the one who lives across the country and visits once a year? Some want to leave equal amounts to each child. Others will decide to give more to their daughter who is a struggling single mother, than to the daughter who is a corporate executive with a six-figure salary. With more and more late marriages, it gets even more complicated. When an 85-year-old marries a 90-year-old, whose children will receive an inheritance? What percentage will each child receive? Will all the assets go to a surviving spouse? These are the types of questions you need to anticipate and try to answer.

YOUR TO-DO LIST

For those of us who grew up with the *Leave It to Beaver* family model, it may take some time to get used to the idea of your daughter choosing to raise her son of a different race by herself, your nephew getting married to another man, or including your ex-spouse in holiday festivities. The important thing to remember is that in most cases, you do have a choice about how to relate to your family. If other family members do not agree with your choice and do not want to maintain lifelong ties, then it is up to you to fortify your own psychological profile to forgive, forget, and seek meaningful relationships elsewhere.

- **Clarify and communicate your money situation:** As with other family issues, there are steps you can take to address existing or anticipated disagreements about money. Start by taking an inventory of all your assets, so you are clear about where they are, and about their value. Clarify which ones are considered to be joint and which ones belong to you as individuals. Based on the inventory, get clear with yourself and your spouse or partner about your priorities for use of the assets. The next step is to talk with your children, or other relevant family members, about the decisions you have made on priorities. It is not necessary to reveal your exact budget. However, you should create a will and other necessary legal documents required to avoid conflict and uncertainty in the future. Be sure to specify who has authority to make financial decisions for you, should you become unable to do so. Then, although it could be difficult, advise family members on the decisions you have made. If your financial situation is complicated or family members have become combative about money, seek appropriate professional help, whether from a financial advisor, a lawyer, or family therapist.

- **Find your relationship safe haven:** One woman reported that her husband was becoming incapacitated. It was difficult for him to go out of the house to restaurants or to participate in other activities. His life was restricted. She had one very close friend who kept in touch on a daily basis, encouraging her to go to movies and plays. Her friend went with her and was her safe haven.
- **Work with a counselor or therapist to help you reframe your situation:** In her 80s, Mona met a man who was also in his 80s. They were having a wonderful time getting to know each other. However, his son was constantly micromanaging his father. He

wanted to see him constantly and confirm that his father was keeping his doctor's appointments. Mona became so aggravated she went to a therapist, who helped her see the situation differently. The man was approaching 85 and his son felt he needed to see his father as much as possible. The therapist helped Mona see that this involvement was reasonable and understandable. As Mona let go of her aggravation, the son was slightly less intrusive.

- **Appreciate your family:** Alice, a 50-year-old woman, did not get along with her 80-year-old mother; yet when Alice was diagnosed with incurable cancer, her mother came to live with her, to nurse and nurture Alice during her last 6 months. This is not always the case, but for many, there are times when family members are the major people we can count on for support. If we can express our gratitude and appreciation for those in our family and be prepared to forgive—although, maybe not forget—we will find a richness of support.

IV

CREATE THE NEW YOU

9

Keep Your Dance Card Full: Pay Attention to Friends, Family, and Fun

George Vaillant, former director of the Harvard study on adult development, wrote in his most recent book, *Triumphs of Experience*, that the most significant finding in the 75-year history of the study is that "the only thing that really matters in life are your relations to other people."[1] The current study director, Robert J. Waldinger, confirmed this finding when he spoke at the TEDxBeaconStreet conference: "It turns out that people who are more socially connected to family, to friends, [and] to community, are happier, they are physically healthier, and they live longer than people who are less well connected. And the experience of loneliness turns out to be toxic."[2]

A recent widow, 72-year-old Nadine, impulsively signed up for a barge trip down the Canal Du Midi in France. She confessed,

> It started with bravado. I decided to take a trip by myself. I presented myself as an adventurer—someone

unafraid. My son was to take me to the airport but at the last minute his baby became ill and she had to be taken to the emergency room. So I took a cab by myself. I felt so alone. I realized I was a total fraud presenting myself as an adventurer. I had stupidly made my own travel arrangements and found out that there were some transfers I did not expect.

On the trip, as a single, I felt alone. Every night I worried about what would happen at dinner. With whom would I eat? I felt shy and did not want to intrude [on others]. The tables were long and set for 8 people. I hesitated to ask to join a table [of three couples] since that would leave [an unoccupied chair at the table]. One couple asked me to join them one night and then said they love eating with new people every night. That was my signal not to ask again.

Despite these negative experiences, Nadine was glad she went on the trip. She found out she could handle being alone (even if it made her uncomfortable) and could manage the unexpected travel inconveniences. She was used to having her husband take care of any difficulties, but now she knew she was competent to do it by herself.

Nadine's experience—feeling alone and lonely— is far from unique. A women's support group has been meeting for 30 years to discuss a variety of topics, mostly related to relationships like being a mother-in-law, a grandmother, or a friend. At one meeting, the topic was loneliness, and the meeting's leader described her experience after she and her husband decided to get a divorce. She felt lonely, empty, and distraught. To assuage her loneliness, she read all she could find on the topic.

As the group discussion progressed, it became clear that for her and other members, the group itself served as a comfort. The members had become close friends. Over the years several members had died, several had lost spouses, and one had lost a son through suicide. They were lonely at times, but their friendship sustained them.

THE CHALLENGE: UNDERSTANDING LONELINESS

Loneliness can strike at any age, but as we get older and lose friends, family, and even community, it is not unusual to experience loneliness and struggle with its effects.

Even though I knew that loneliness takes an enormous toll, it was not until I read Robert Weiss's book, *Loneliness: The Experience of Emotional and Social Isolation*, that I was able to understand my own and others' experiences. Weiss identified two different forms of loneliness resulting from what he labeled *relational deficit*.[3] The first, loneliness from emotional isolation, arises when an intimate relationship is interrupted by death or other problems. Many people can relate to this form of loneliness. One woman expressed it this way: "When my husband died after 50 years of marriage, I felt bereft." The second, loneliness from social isolation, is a break in one's social network. This too is something many of us have experienced. A CEO of a nonprofit organization expressed it as follows:

> For years, I felt very much part of my community largely because I was an active player. I felt that I mattered to the community. Unfortunately, the organization I led

failed. Since then there have been several new initiatives to develop programs and I have not been invited to be part of those. I have lost that part of my social network.

Another dimension of relational deficit relates to the death of contemporaries. One woman looked at a picture of a birthday party given to her on her 70th birthday by her women friends. Today, three are dead, two are in nursing homes, and two have moved. In other words, the group she considered to be her close friends no longer exists.

Caregivers are particularly at risk for loneliness. One man described his emotional isolation. His wife does not appreciate what he does for her and becomes angry with him. Another caregiver expressed social isolation:

> There is another piece that no one's talked about. It is the loss of friends. We have all experienced it; people that you shared things with are not there anymore. The circle of everyday social friends is shrinking. They do not ask to have coffee anymore.

Other at-risk groups include new widows and widowers, people who are newly retired, and newcomers to a community. Anyone who loses an intimate relationship and/or a social network of friends is also at risk. Even people who are married or are part of a group can feel marginal and unhappy. If a marriage is unsatisfactory, but before one declares it is time to end it, one can feel very isolated.

In his article "All the Lonely People," Brad Edmondson reviewed data from a survey of AARP members, and concluded that we are in the midst of a loneliness epidemic. "Thirty-five percent are chronically lonely . . . compared with 20% . . . a decade ago," he wrote. He pointed out that loneliness is "an equal opportunity affliction" that can be experienced by people in all types of environments; it can also compromise one's physical health. Edmondson referred to the work of John T. Cacioppo, director of the Center for Cognitive and Social Neuroscience at the University of Chicago. "Loneliness has surprisingly broad and profound health effects. . . . There is mounting evidence that loneliness significantly increases the chances of diabetes, sleep disorders, and other potentially life-threatening problems."[4]

ATTACHMENT THEORY AND OLDER PEOPLE: SURVIVING YOUR PEERS AND FACING BEING ALONE

Psychologist John Bowlby, renowned for his work on attachment theory, showed that when the connection between infants and parents is weak, or broken, infants can be psychologically damaged. The importance of the attachment bond is critical to healthy development.[5] Some scholars have extended attachment theory to explain the continued bond between adult children and parents, suggesting that when adult attachment relationships are broken sadness, depression, and loneliness can follow.[6] That is one reason it is so important to have lots of connections—some intimate and some casual—to protect against social or emotional isolation.

So what happens when you are the last of your family, your golf group, or your high school crowd? Many older people claim that the main thing they dislike about aging is that all their contemporaries die. When you reach this point, you begin to face your own mortality.

One retired artist told a story about how she coped with outliving her many older friends. In her late 60s, she began realizing that it was likely that eventually she would lose some or all of them. She consciously decided to gather younger people and start a game group. She invited 10 people to her house; they all came and are still coming once a month to play games like Password, Scrabble, and Charades. She looks forward to those evenings and feels a real bond with each group member.

As with the artist, there is no denying that as we age, we experience losses, including some through death. As our friends die, it makes us think more about what we can do to enhance the time we have left and about the choices we may face at the end.

PUMP UP YOUR SOCIAL LIFE

We can all point to our own experiences, or the experiences of others, and identify loneliness. But the more important question is, what, if anything, can you do about it? Fortunately, there are answers: You can develop, diversify, and rebalance your social contacts and activities; take advantage of social media tools; and take time for fun.

Maintain Your Social Supports

Our social supports change over time and include friends, siblings, family, lovers, spouses, and acquaintances. The specifics are not as important as the need to have relationships that includes intimate relationships like best friends, lovers, or close family, as well as meaningful people in your life and casual acquaintances. At times, your sibling may be your best friend, at other times he or she may be in your outer circle. One woman, who was very active in her community, complained that she was very lonely even though she was busy—sometimes too busy. She experienced loneliness because she no longer had a best friend. Robert Kahn and Toni Antonucci developed a way to identify your potential supports by drawing a series of concentric circles with you at the center. Imagine the circle closest to you contains your closest, most intimate friends and family, who are presumably part of your life forever. The next circle is for family, friends, and neighbors who are important in your life but not in the same intimate way as the first group. The circle furthest away from you represents institutional supports. Kahn and Antonucci called these circles an individual's "convoy of social support."[7] Your convoy endures throughout your lifetime, but the people in each circle change.

By mapping your supports this way, you can visualize how your support system has changed over time. For example, common circumstances that prompt our support systems to change include retirement, a geographical move, illness, or a death. If a newly retired couple moves away from many supports to a place where they have none, the transition may be very difficult. If, however, retirement liberates one or both spouses to return to an area where there are intimate relatives and friends, then the transition might be much easier. One recently retired woman bemoaned the fact that the people with whom she had interacted daily, with whom she had coffee and shared gossip, were no longer in her life. She was wondering how to identify a substitute community.

This image of concentric circles shows that the most important aspect of a transition may not be the change itself but what it does to the individual's convoy.

This is particularly relevant for those who have lost people in their inner circle. One woman lost her husband and two best friends in the same year. Her inner circle was diminished. Although she had many friends and acquaintances in the outer circles, she was lonely for the intimacy she had had with her husband and best friends. Her task was to figure out how to substitute for these losses.

Nurture Your Friendships

Friends are freely chosen. Lillian Rubin, author of *Just Friends*, wrote, "friendship is experienced as a conditional relationship, kinship as an unconditional one . . . friends choose to do what kin are obliged to do." She suggested that friendship is an all-inclusive term that does not distinguish between a casual acquaintance, a close friend, or a best friend. It is interesting that Facebook, a major social medium, allows members to categorize their contacts as friends, close friends, or acquaintances. She wrote, "To study friendship . . . is to trip over the ambiguity, ambivalence, contradiction, and paradox with which this subject is hedged in our society . . . I shall argue also that friends are central actors in the continuing developmental drama of our adulthood."[8]

A groundbreaking UCLA study, reported by Gale Berkowitz, illustrated the importance of women's friendships—how women "tend and befriend." Friends contribute to reducing stress and living longer. In fact, it was found that when women lose their husbands, if they have a confidante, they will get through loss and sometimes even thrive.[9]

Use Social Media for Social Support

Lisbeth, grandmother of a 4-year-old and a 6-year-old, uses email to stay in touch with her grandchildren, who live more than a thousand miles away. She and her husband used to use Skype to speak with their children but found later that it was easier to use FaceTime, as it can be operated on a cell phone rather than a desktop computer. The use of electronic communication to stay in touch with children and grandchildren makes a lot of sense; most of the younger generation have adapted to new the technologies and are not in the habit of writing letters or spending hours on the telephone. When Lisbeth requested a wish list of birthday presents, the 6-year-old responded by sending a text with a photo of two plastic dinosaurs.

The technology of the 21st century has provided us with a whole series of new tools for developing and maintaining social ties, as well as ways to meet new friends and find romance. Older adults use social media for three main reasons: to reconnect with people from their past, to seek out support groups and/or information for chronic diseases, and to bridge generational gaps and foster connections with family and friends.[10]

It all started with email, which continues to be an important way for older adults to stay in touch with family and friends who live far away. A 2010 study by the Pew Research Center found that "92% of those ages 50–64, and 89% of those ages 65 and older, send or read email and more than half of each group exchanges email messages on a typical day." The study also found that substantial numbers of older adults use the Internet to gather news, which is a way of staying in touch with the world around you.[11]

More recently, older adults have joined the social media bandwagon, signing up for and using sites like Facebook, LinkedIn, and Twitter in growing numbers. Some 81% of older adults who use social networking sites say that they socialize with others (either in person, online, or over the telephone) on a daily or near-daily basis.[12]

However, attention must be paid to the difficulties some older adults face when it comes to using new technologies. In the past month, four older adults have asked me to help them meet a companion online. However, they (a) did not own computers and (b) were afraid of technology. Despite the enormous increase in senior use, there are still many older adults who either cannot afford computers or who are afraid to use them.

Take Time for Fun

Dr. Gene Cohen, author of *The Mature Mind*, reviewed the literature on the relationship of positive mental and physical health to social engagement. He pointed out the importance of diversifying and balancing your activities. To do that, he urged people to pay attention to what he called the *social portfolio*.[13] This portfolio includes solitary activities, like writing a memoir, and group endeavors, like tennis, dancing, and participating in a book club.

Sigmund Freud wrote that work and love are central tasks that challenge adults. I would add play to the mix. Play, a spontaneous free-spirited activity, can be fun. We live in a serious world, and it is a relief to play games like golf, tennis, or backgammon, unless you take a game so seriously and become so competitive that it is no longer fun. In other words, we need freedom to think and behave in new ways—to become creative. It is important to remain open to trying new activities, including those you may have thought were only appropriate for "younger folks."

One way a lot of people have fun in later life is by dancing, which has the additional benefit of being good physical exercise. One man reported that the secret of his feeling young was dancing with his companion. Many fitness centers and community programs offer options including tap, ballroom, and line dancing. The events also provide an opportunity for retired musicians to play music.

The following example comes from Ellen Hoffman, author of "Rewards of Dancing as You Age," who described how, at age 71, she incorporated a new type of fun into her life: dancing. Here's what she wrote, in an abridged version of an article that originally appeared on Nextavenue.org. It is reprinted with permission.[14]

> My partner Riccardo is a good dancer who loves salsa and rock and roll (but says "I will dance to anything with a beat"). For more than 20 years he tried to cajole me onto the dance floor. . . . I always felt I was a terrible dancer. . . . So when we stopped in La Crosse [a small Wisconsin town] the night before going on to spend a month in my hometown of Minneapolis, Minnesota, last year, Riccardo pretty much had to drag me into the grungy local bar with an ear-splitting band and an empty dance floor. By the time we left a couple of hours later a much younger local was impressed enough to say "you guys really cut some rug. I can tell you were really there in the '60s."

Although I did not realize it at the time, that night may have been my first inkling that there could be an upside to this business of seniors dancing in public. Ever since, it has become increasingly evident to me that, in addition to providing physical exercise, dancing can offer other dividends including intergenerational, cultural, and geographical connections.

The live music/dance venues in Minneapolis got started and ended too late for us. But when we got home, we were returning to a small town with a lot of bands and local musicians, to say nothing of a vintage opera house-turned-concert venue, with a small dance floor, right down the street from us.

Almost every weekend now we can be found on a dance floor somewhere. I will not say I am totally over my hesitation, but I have realized there is no shame in not knowing the latest formal steps, because everyone pretty much creates their own moves in response to the rock, bluegrass, blues, and related permutations of music that are popular here.

Along with the revelation that you can do almost any step you want, has come a rewarding sense of just plain good vibes—an amazing sense of support that for me, anyway, has helped overcome my fear of making a fool of myself in public at my advanced age.

In fact, it seems that mainly because of our respective ages of 71 and 77, Riccardo and I have gained a certain notoriety for our willingness to join the . . . crowd on the dance floors of various venues.

One night . . . as we arrived at the Shepherdstown (West Virginia) Opera House, a young man . . . called out to us: "Are you going to dance up a storm tonight?" Another night, as the band was packing up and we were leaving, another young man . . . said, "You guys are the best, oldest dancers . . ."

[Some] nights . . . the dance floor is so crowded [we] can hardly move. On those occasions, we inevitably find ourselves surrounded both by younger friends and by what I might call "dancing acquaintances." When they see us on the dance floor, they sashay up to hug us or to shimmy around us, their arms raised high over their heads, or to gently pull us into a circle dance.

Because Riccardo and I spend a lot of time in Argentina, we started taking tango classes. But after realizing how difficult it is to learn, we went AWOL after a few sessions. On the other hand, in Argentina, we also learned the lesson that pure form is not always the path to the rewards of dancing.

A case in point occurred on a balmy summer evening [at a Caribbean dance fest in Argentina] . . . when we were one of the first couples (apparently the only nonlocals) on the outdoor dance floor, and we stuck it out—while admiring the form of our fellow dancers who had impressively mastered the mambo, the cha-cha, and other Caribbean rhythms—until the very end.

As the master of ceremonies approached the stage to say farewell to the audience, we started to leave, making our way across the lawn. Suddenly we realized a young woman was running and calling after us. "Come back, come back," she said. "You have won a prize!"

Somewhat dazed, we followed her back to the podium, where we were asked to step up to receive a bottle of Mendoza wine as recognition of—not our dancing style—but our *endurance*. The award was for spending more time on the dance floor than any other couple.[15]

Your To-Do List

This chapter has been about how to overcome the loss of friends, family, and routines in your life to build new, rewarding social relationships. Identifying your social supports, consciously seeking new ones through friendship, and taking time to have fun or for romance, are all important, broad strategies.

Implementing them can take time, and it can also be helpful to take some baby steps to arrive at your own solutions. The following are some specific tips to set you on the path.

- **Study the topic:** The leader of the women's group who talked about her loneliness after a divorce said the first thing she did was to read everything she could on the subject. In addition to books, the Internet may also be a good source of information.
- **Increase your emotional connections as a way to overcome emotional isolation:** If you have lost your most intimate connection, take time to grieve. Join a grief group. Talk about it with a therapist. Over time, start looking for a new attachment figure. Let others know you are looking. More and more people of all ages are going online to meet someone special.
- **Increase your social connections:** One woman, recently widowed but lonely for several years as she cared for a spouse with Parkinson's disease, joined a temple. The rabbi and membership welcomed her.

She has become very active and is totally absorbed with contributing to and benefiting from being part of this community. Identify an organization and offer to volunteer. Become engaged.

- **Think about your social circle or convoy:** Try to make sure you have people with whom you are intimate, as well as good friends and family, plus lots of acquaintances. We all need a confidante as well as a social network. We need to fill up our dance cards.

- **Start networking:** Malcolm Gladwell underscored the importance of connecting through "strong ties," where you would find jobs or dates through personal connections, and "weak ties," with people you barely know. Both are critical, but if you are only using strong ties, you probably already know the same people. It is through weak ties that you meet people and groups you did not previously know.[16]

As we age, we may lose friends and family to relocation, illness, or death. It is important to keep our social network growing. We need all types of relationships—close friends, acquaintances, family, and lovers. Throughout life, even as we age and find the logistics of "getting out" more difficult, it is important to engage with other people. This chapter affirms the need to nurture our relationships with others, and just as we do with our financial portfolio, we need to diversify and work to expand our social portfolio.

10

Go for Romance (If You Want It)

Does Saturday night have to be the loneliest night of the week? For some people, it is not enough to go out dancing or to dinner with a group of friends; they want intimacy and romance in their lives.

Does everyone want romance? Therapist, Paul Weiss, who ran a support group for men between the ages of 60 and 75, reported that sex and romance were major issues for his members. A group of women in their 70s and 80s meet regularly to talk about their dating lives. They laugh, giggle, and report that they feel like teenagers. Although there are similarities between these older women and their teenage selves, there are a few differences. In their teen years, they were worried about pregnancy, but in old age, they are concerned about AIDS. So we can see that romance, and the need for it, has no age limits.

According to the U.S. Census Bureau, "During the 20th century, the number of persons in the United States under age 65 has tripled . . . and the number age

65 or over has jumped by a factor of 11." Those over 85 are the fastest-growing group, and at this age women outnumber men five to two.[1] One woman told her ailing husband, "You have to fight to stay alive. You are demographically irreplaceable."

Our stereotypes of the social life of aging men and women often include shuffleboard, watching TV, and dining on early-bird specials, but not first dates, romance, or sexual encounters. However, the numbers of older adults engaging in romance are on the rise. Deborah Todd, a reporter for the *Pittsburgh Post-Gazette*, found that "seniors . . . are looking for companionship, and many are looking for a partner to spend the rest of their lives with."[2] Individuals may have different reasons for seeking an intimate partner in their life: to offer comfort and security, to serve as a close friend, or even marriage. A study by the AARP, "Lifestyles, Dating, and Romance: A Study of Midlife Singles," pinpointed some gender differences: Women typically want companionship and men typically want both companionship and sex. Whatever need is to be fulfilled, having a special relationship beyond close friends and family is important for many older adults.[3]

Of course, not all older people are interested in long-term, intimate relationships. Women tend to live longer than men, which leads to a greater number of women than men among older adults. These women seem to fall in three groups: those disinterested in dating or romance, those interested but not seeking, and those actively seeking romance. One woman summed up her disinterest by saying, "I am through with pots and pans and prostate glands." For those who are open to encountering romance or for those who choose to seek it out, a number of issues arise and should be considered before forging ahead.

ELEPHANTS IN THE ROOM

Couples who plunge into late-life romance—regardless of whether they live together or marry—have to deal with sex, children's reactions to their search for intimacy and romance, and concerns about illness and caregiving.

Sex

This is clearly the biggest elephant in the room. One 82-year-old man exclaimed that he is now a sex object— women are coming on to him all the time. He seems amused and pleased about it. Mel, a 70-year-old widower, explained that one barrier to his dating, especially with younger women, is that he cannot always perform sexually because of health issues. He said his wife understood, but he worries that if any other women entered his life down the road, it would be a potential stumbling block.

In general, men worry more about being impotent and women worry more about how their bodies look when they undress. Many women agree that sex would have to be in total darkness, at least in the beginning. On the other hand, some people are happy making a conscious decision to keep a relationship platonic. Amy, who is in her 70s, met a man through political activities and sees him exclusively, but they have no intention of living together and they have agreed to forego sex. They like their platonic relationship.

Men and women interested in the "how to" of sex in their later years can check out the AARP website (http://www.aarp.org). In addition, several writers discuss the pros and cons of Viagra, sex without intercourse, and other matters of interest.[4]

Children

Children's reactions to their parents' search for romance can be another elephant in the room. Mark became agitated when he realized his mother was dating. He was worried that someone would take advantage of her, give her bad advice, or even scam her. He knew someone who had started dating in her 60s, met a man, married him, and then found out that "he was a scoundrel" who had been sleeping with other women. She divorced him, but continued to wear her wedding ring so men would assume she was married.

Children may also be afraid that the inheritance they expected from their parents will be diverted to a new love interest, or that their parents will not have as much time for them or their grandchildren. Whatever the fears, adult children can interfere with their parents' romantic lives. One man felt that his relationship with a woman was delayed from proceeding smoothly because her children were protective of their mother. Another man felt that part of the reason for his breakup with a woman was her adult children's financial and emotional needs for their mother's attention. On the other hand, many children are delighted that their parents have found someone. It relieves them of worry and makes them happy.

Illness and Caregiving

Concern about late-life illness may be another reason some older people do not want to marry or make a life-long commitment. Marriage, of course, is a commitment through "sickness and health," and it confers certain legal rights and obligations. But what happens if one member, or even both members, of the couple become seriously ill or disabled? This situation can cause family and economic problems, especially when the marriage is not the first. For example, a widower remarried when he was in his 80s. In his early 90s his wife, who was a few years younger, developed signs of serious dementia (e.g., leaving the stove on). He could not leave her alone in the apartment for fear of accidents. Although he was relatively healthy for his age and totally sharp mentally, it became impossible for him to assume the full responsibility of caring for her while living in an apartment building with no services for seniors. In addition, he did not have the resources to hire caregivers. When he suggested to her two adult children that perhaps they could assist with some caregiving, they denied that she needed care, and refused to help. Shortly thereafter, the children arrived at the apartment, announced that they were moving their mother out, and began to remove her furniture. The upshot, of course, was an unpleasant divorce settlement that had to be negotiated with the unfriendly children. The children placed their mother in yet another apartment without adequate care; she had to be moved again to a special facility.

Similar dilemmas can even arise when couples have a close relationship but have not comingled their finances or decided to cohabit. One 80-year-old man expressed relief that he and his woman friend had not moved in together; when she developed dementia, her children took over.

THE MANY FORMS OF ROMANCE

Romance and intimacy can take many forms. *Companionship* can include dating and friendship; *living-apart together* can mean a committed, often sexual, relationship, in which the couple lives separately but vacations and/or spends a lot of time together; and *living together* typically refers to couples who cohabitate but do not have a legal relationship; and *'til death do us part* includes legal marriage. As people live longer, new forms of romantic relationships continue to evolve, posing issues that our parents and grandparents probably did not have to address.

Loretta, a widow, found herself worrying about being lonely on Valentine's Day: "I am in my 70s, attractive, enthusiastic, and fun. I had a really happy marriage and want to find a man with whom to share my life while I am still healthy. I am not sure how to proceed."

Loretta told me that she knew three women who were in recent relationships with men "but have made a conscious decision not to marry and not to live together." The expectation in each case is that the relationship will be an exclusive one. These couples socialize with other friends but they are not dating others and do not have other romantic relationships. But rituals (e.g., spending time during the holidays) may vary because these couples are not married, and their expectations, as well as their families', are not the same as if they were married. For example, Natalie, considering Thanksgiving with her group of friends, said, "Only one of the couples [I know] will be together this year. One man is with his daughter in the same city; [another] man is traveling out of town to be with family."

Other issues, such as nagging, can arise in these types of fluid relationships. One woman started to point out things she thought needed changing in her friend's apartment. His response was that maybe they should spend all their time in her apartment. He added, however, "I am a bachelor with a dog," pointing out that at least in the current stage of their relationship, there were boundaries.

One woman complains that her companion does not sleep over; they have sex, but he goes home afterward, and they rarely travel together. Another says that her "friend" sometimes sleeps at her house, but she is not sure in advance when that will happen. "We travel together and sleep at each other's apartments depending on what we are doing," she explains.

Couples who are dating but not married or living together do not have any outward symbol representing their status. Somehow, when you are married or living together, there is an assumption that you are "in love." But one man skirted the issue, suggesting he and his companion were "in like"—a state that is more than just "liking" each other but not yet akin to the young love that leads to marriage.

For some people, these undefined relationships can be positive, offering friendship and companionship but also freedom and space. However, this kind of ambiguous relationship can also produce insecurity.

Committed Relationships: Together but Apart

One of the twists and turns that relationships take in the older years is to make a strong personal commitment but not share a living space. This is what happened with Betty and Bill, who knew each other when they were previously married to other people. Then they both lost their spouse within the same year. Coincidentally, Betty had just moved into the retirement community where Bill and his wife had lived. Before long, they started eating dinner together. Bill wanted to get serious; Betty hesitated, but as time went on, she became equally committed. She felt very lucky. "All we do is play," she explained, "I feel like a teenager all over again." Bill added, "When my wife died, I felt so alone." These days, although they live in separate apartments, neither of them feels alone.

At age 60, Joe became a caregiver for his partner, Paul, of 30 years. When Paul died, Joe grieved for the end of this long-standing relationship. His friends and family rallied around, but Joe was very lonely not just for Paul, but for a relationship. At the encouragement of friends, he registered at an online site for gay men. One of his first dates, Don, was a perfect match. They have been together for 2 years, living-apart together. For example, one weekend they visited Joe's father, and the next weekend they went to visit Don's mother. Joe's experience can be instructive for older people. Although we experience loss, renewal is often possible.

Marriage

There are many late-life marriages. According to the Pew Research Center, about 53% of Americans age 55 and older are remarried. In other words, many older adults are on their second or third marriage. This large number also comprises same-sex marriages, which are becoming more common.[5]

Mary Ann, a 65-year-old widow, kept in touch with the friend who introduced her to her late husband. Last October, that friend invited her to Hilton Head Island, South Carolina, for a 6-day visit. Mary Ann's friend did not mention that she had also invited a 75-year-old widower, John, and another couple. Soon after the vacation, John called Mary Ann to confess, "I am too old to waste time, so if you are interested, I would love to see you again." They soon arranged for John to visit from a neighboring state.

Mary Ann described how nervous she was when she and John met again. Trying to hide her anxiety, she kept "jumping up and down, getting things from the kitchen, and taking walks when John was resting." The weekend was followed by many more as she and John developed a nice friendship. "I felt I could trust him, and we shared similar values," she explained. Early in the relationship "he would kiss me on the cheek, with an occasional hug. The turning point came several months later when we were invited to a party. That night he gave me a romantic kiss. I have not had feelings like this since I was a teenager." Mary Ann was not looking for romance but is absolutely thrilled to have found "true love" at her stage of life. The relationship escalated; they became engaged, to give their children time to get used to the notion of their parents remarrying, and remarried the following year.

Making Connections

You do not necessarily have to go on a dating spree to find a compatible partner, but to be successful you will have to think creatively and positively, and be open to opportunities that present themselves.

People meet in all kinds of expected and unexpected ways—through shared activities, at the checkout counter, in an elevator, at a political event, at a dinner party, in a retirement community, through friends, on Facebook, and through online dating and matchmaking sites. "I never expected to meet someone special and certainly did not think my daughter would be my matchmaker," exclaimed one woman. Another woman said, "Going online has a negative connotation. It implies that you could not get someone on your own. And you really do not know the background of those you are meeting."

Leah, a woman in her early 70s, was skeptical but finally succumbed to a friend's encouragement and registered with a popular online dating site. She found it amusing that people presented themselves online in unrealistic ways. She noted that there was a great deal of exaggeration in the profiles—short people said they were tall, fat people underestimated their weight. Resisting the temptation to "polish up" her own profile, Leah told the truth about her age and her weight. She also wrote that she liked to travel first-class. As a result, she received many messages from men in their 30s who thought she was rich and would take care of them.

Despite her reservations, Leah met someone of an appropriate age who "looked stylish." He was a great fit! She arranged to meet him in a bar; one of her friends also went to the same bar for security. They met and got along. Now he would like her to commit to a lifetime relationship, but she is happy seeing each other exclusively and not living together.

Some couples who meet on the Internet still prefer marriage. Molly, age 90, and Ed, age 82, met online.

Molly said, "I knew a knight on a white horse would not come and sweep me off my feet. I knew if I wanted something to happen, I would have to do something about it." She posted her profile on Match.com, even though she felt foolish doing it. It worked. Ed responded to her profile, and they found they both loved scotch and Shakespeare.[6]

There are a number of online dating sites geared to older people. You can find them by searching for terms such as "senior dating sites," "online dating for seniors," or "top dating sites for seniors." On all sites that cater to older adults, women outnumber men, and most ask users to specify the age range of people in whom they are interested. Many men specify interest in younger women, and many men and women lie about their ages.

It is important to remember, however, that anytime you engage online with people you do not know, there can be risks. One woman shared her story: As a result of signing up on a dating site she was "stalked by four separate people." "It was distressing," she said, "at least the first time, and then I got very smart about reading any posts." Older adults are especially vulnerable to scams on online dating sites.

The scale of online dating by seniors has not been formally researched, and most of the information available is anecdotal. But because the trend is obvious, the Pew Research Center is planning to launch a major survey on the topic. And the stigma of meeting online is disappearing. I am one of those who, after trying other ways to meet a new life partner, made the decision that going online would not compromise my reputation or my view of myself.

FINDING LOVE AGAIN: MY STORY

Years ago, it never would have occurred to me that when I was in my 80s, I would be writing about dating and romance. But researching and writing an article for a magazine on senior romance a year after my husband died made me begin to think romance, even love, was possible at any age. I was ready for a love affair, but my friends' fix-ups and my own contacts were not working out, so I had to take more aggressive steps.

Once I admitted my interest in romance, I had a number of dates. One man lived in another city, another man's wife had Alzheimer's disease, another man was too boring, and the two men I found most promising found me resistible. Everyone said I was lucky to have dates, but I felt sad and lonely that I did not have a relationship. Dates I was getting; romance was elusive. I started telling all my friends that I would love to meet someone, but only one person could think of someone who seemed appropriate.

"How do the men get grabbed up so quickly, and what are other women doing that I do not know about?" I wondered. (I knew I could not join the Casserole Brigade because I do not cook.) Then it occurred to me—there was something I could do. My son met his wife online. Would that work for me? Obviously, my immediate circle could not help me. I was afraid of searching for romance online, so I went to Google and searched for a matchmaking service.

Impulsively, I invested too much money in what appeared to be a first-class service. After many conversations with the owner and the service's psychologist in the course of a year, I had not received a single contact. I later discovered that the organization had been sued and had declared bankruptcy. My backup plan was to conquer my fear and join five online dating services. My friend checked my profile and thought it reflected me. I made it clear that I was politically liberal; a writer who was active in my community; and not the type who would cook, clean, or sew. I spent time every night checking the sites and enjoyed the process. I corresponded with a 91-year-old man about transitions, flirted with many others, and responded to a 60-year-old man who wanted to meet me, although I told him I thought 60 was too young for an 83-year-old woman.

Then, through an online site I met Ron, a widower who was living in the same city as me, and we began emailing. Eventually, I gave him my phone number and we began talking on the phone. We made plans to meet for lunch after several weeks. He suggested that he pick me up for the date. I was hesitant to let a stranger pick me up at home, but after he persisted, I said, "You can pick me up if you assure me that you are not a murderer or a rapist." He assured me! I gave a friend all of the information I had about Ron and suggested that if she did not hear from me by 4 p.m., she should call out the troops.

Ron and I started seeing each other—slowly at first. We got along well. When my internist found out I was dating an 86-year-old man she said, "You must promise me that you will not go to bed with him until he has a test for AIDS." And furthermore, she argued, "I will give you a blood test so you can show him you are clear of AIDS." I explained that it was highly unlikely that I could have AIDS, having been married for 48 years in a monogamous, committed relationship. However, what my doctor was telling me was that if I showed my stamp of approval to Ron, then he would be more likely to get cleared.

Can you picture my discussing this sensitive topic with my new friend? First of all, we had not begun a sexual relationship. So how was I to suggest he be tested for AIDS? I began very broadly: "Have you heard of the AIDS epidemic among the elderly?" He had not and I tried to alarm him about this, adding, "Well, I would never have sex with someone who had not been tested." He emailed me the next day saying he could not wait to see his doctor. However, when I casually asked later if he had seen his doctor, he said no but he would if I insisted. I am not sure if he ever had the test.

My doctor had also told me I could have sex if my partner used a condom. It amazed me to think that an 86-year-old man would be able to maintain an erection long enough to put on a condom. Since I was not sure about his abilities in this area, I decided not to mention this possibility. When Ron invited me to his home in the Adirondacks, a friend gave me a birthday present before I went—a book, written by a psychologist, called *Getting Naked Again*.[7]

Ron and I continued to see each other, and after a year, he and his dog moved in with me. After living together for another year, we decided we were ready to downsize and relocate in a retirement community that offered comfort and a variety of services.

When I look back, I see that my focus in life underwent a series of transitions over a period of years, shifting from caregiving and anticipating my husband's death, to becoming a widow, to having many dates and experiencing many disappointments, to finally embracing Internet dating and meeting someone with whom I hope to have a long, loving relationship.

YOUR TO-DO LIST

My personal and my professional experience tell me that there are some needs that are common to people of all ages—the need to matter to someone else, the need to love and be loved, and the need to be appreciated. To make these things happen, it is necessary to consider the following.

■ **Identify your connectors:** These are people you know with whom you can discuss your interest in meeting someone else.

- **Use social media:** It can be a good way to access people you do not know.
- **Participate in community organizations and activities.**
- **Be patient:** Realize that every contact does not produce immediate success. Sometimes it takes contacting two or three connectors. It is a "what is next" strategy that can work. Do not let Saturday be the loneliest night in the week.

11

Create Your Own Happiness:
Your Path to Positive Aging

On the one hand, many of us feel young inside; on the other, it's hard to ignore an almost constant stream of negative comments—many focused on the mental and physical decline—about the aging process. Harry Moody, retired vice president of AARP and father of the positive aging movement, put this contradiction in perspective in his *Human Values Newsletter:* "We love 'happy talk' about aging: successful aging, productive aging positive aging. But are we willing to tell the truth, or better, face the truth, if the truth includes the shadow as well as the light."[1]

This book is not meant to deny or sugarcoat the losses and sadness that can accompany aging. Rather, it presents an alternative way of approaching aging, called *positive aging*. As one woman said, "I might not be able to be always optimistic but I can aspire to be upbeat while accepting the losses and dismissive way older people are often—not always—treated."

As we age, we inevitably experience a series of transitions, positive and negative. Many are new challenges, and often these are related to the fact that, on average, we are living longer than our parents, grandparents, and the generations that came before them. For this reason, many of us face the transitions of aging without a clear path to mastering them.

In the chapters of this book, we examined a number of transitions, including retirement, location, health, family, friends, and romance. What these transitions have in common is that they usually have a concrete date, or at least a general time, when they happened. You retired in 2009, you became a widow or a widower in 2011, and you moved to a new town in 2012. However, we also face subtler transitions, like changes in our identity, ambitions, and well-being. These generally occur over a period of months or years, and we may not even recognize the changes as they occur.

AS THE KALEIDOSCOPE TURNS, SO DOES YOUR PERSPECTIVE

A kaleidoscope can serve as a metaphor for viewing our life transitions. At a conference on transitions, each participant was given a bookmark and a set of colored pencils. At the top of the bookmark was a black-and-white drawing of a kaleidoscope. Each participant was asked to color in the kaleidoscope. The black-and-white graphic illustrated the structure that can be applied to any transition, but each individual's kaleidoscope differed. That's the point: Transitions are dynamic. One of the most critical coping strategies is understanding your transition and then trying to see it in a new light. Each time we twist the lens of the kaleidoscope, we see a new configuration, a changed landscape requiring a new vision and new way of being in the world. Often people discuss transitions as a linear progression with a beginning, middle, and end. The kaleidoscope reflects the nature of transitions more accurately—as different colors with different hues and intensity. You have the power to turn the kaleidoscope, which opens up new configurations and new colors of the transition. If you allow it, you can see life in a new way.

Consider the following examples of people who were able to turn their kaleidoscope and view their life in a different way. A 90-year-old woman started seeing her physical ability in a different light. Despite several bouts of cancer, she was able to play nine holes of golf with her son. She was amazed that she could do it, and it made her feel wonderful. Another woman in her 70s decided to stop defining herself as shy. She took a course in public speaking as a way to conquer her shyness, and it worked. A man in his 80s pushed aside his fear of flying and booked a ticket to travel around the world. He realized he was acting "old;" he decided that if he did not take the trip now, when would he do it? So, he started to adventure.

The possibilities are endless—with each new activity, with each new turn of the kaleidoscope, you begin to feel "too young to be old."

Your Changing Identity

The transition to defining yourself as old is gradual. No longer am I the youngest member in the department at Wayne State University, no longer am I a middle-aged professor at the University of Maryland; I have become someone who is chronologically old, but someone who is psychologically too young to be old.

For one person, the changing identity may relate to using hearing aids, whereas for another it may be giving up a driver's license. Jessie expressed anxiety about her forthcoming 70th birthday, which is occurring at the same time she is preparing to sell her business. When the business is gone, she will have to shed her professional identity, and she wonders who she will become. Each transition forces us to rethink who we are.

Older people are sometimes compared to adolescents—they experience joy, excitement, misery, anger, love, longings, loneliness, and happiness. They can feel one way today and a different way tomorrow. It reminds me of the Disney/Pixar movie *Inside Out*, in which a young girl experiences many different emotions as she deals with her parents' move to a new community. Her emotions of Joy, Anger, Disgust, Fear, and Sadness are represented by cartoon figures. There is constant interplay of these emotions as Joy tries to return to the control center, so she can manage the young girl's emotions—to avoid negative emotions and return the young girl to a joyous state. In a similar way, this represents what one older adult reported: "As an older person, I get excited about new ventures, feel irrelevant when my voice is no longer heard, and fear when I think about the future, especially loneliness and death. Most of the time my control center moderates the extremes."

Ruthellen Josselson, professor of clinical psychology at the Fielding Graduate University and author of *Finding Herself: Pathways to Identity Development in Women*, discussed identity as "the stable, consistent, and reliable sense of who one is . . . [it] is also a way of preserving the continuity of self."[2] There are two parts to identity—how you see yourself and how others see you.

In some cases, the identity issue surfaces because the older person recognizes a change in how he or she is regarded by others. Author Roger Angell, himself in his 90s, wrote about "the invisibility factor [and how] you've had your turn," meaning that society is no longer interested in what you do or how you think.[3] A 75-year-old man described the phenomenon this way: "I am what you might call *superannuated*; [I am] no longer seen as a player, but as an observer. For those of us with energy we still want to be players, but more and more I realize I am irrelevant."

Changing Ambitions

All too often we allow age bias—our own and others'—to limit our sense of what is possible as we get older. All too often we allow age bias—our own and others'—to limit our sense of what is possible as we get older. Rather than giving up on our ambitions, we should find a way to replace them with satisfying new ones.

One woman said, "I am still on an achievement trajectory, and that is not realistic. I am still hoping to have one of my paintings hung in a permanent museum collection. But the reality is that I have reached the peak and have gone as far as I am going. But inside, I still want that. So why not focus on all that I have done [and] forget what has not happened? I still need to have projects, be engaged, but [I need to] change my sights." In his book, *Ambition: How We Manage Success and Failure Throughout Our Lives*, Orville Brim suggested that to be happy as we age, we need to modify our ambitions.[4] One woman had a career writing for national publications and audiences. As she aged, that opportunity ended and she began writing for a local magazine. She changed her ambitions and was happy with her new place in the writing world.

After retirement, a leading educator decided to follow his avocation of playing the piano. He goes on jazz cruises with his wife, plays when they open up the session to passengers, and plays in the condo where he lives. He does not play jazz professionally, but he is still very much a player.

By way of contrast, consider the example of one woman who refused to lower her ambition goals. She took up professional ballroom dance after she retired and then became a volunteer fundraiser for several nonprofit organizations. After 10 years of fundraising, she claimed "I plan to reinvent myself" and decided to stage a comeback in dance. Now in her 80s, she is working with her partner 5 days a week and traveling around the country to participate in minor competitions in preparation for the big one that she expects to win.

Changing Views of Well-Being

Each one of us can inventory our strengths and limitations, continue to do and live as we want, slow down the pace if necessary, but not give up. Our sense of well-being includes our evaluation of our physical health, our relationships, and our legacy.

Changes in our health status often present challenges as we age. But remember what we discussed in Chapter 7 on health challenges—it is our subjective assessment of our health, just as much as the objective assessment, that makes the difference. Another aspect of our well-being is our social engagement. Are we content with the quality and quantity of our friends, our activities, and our place in the community? If we are, then we will experience feelings of well-being. If living close to family has always been a priority for you, your sense of well-being may suffer if your children and grandchildren decide to move hundreds of miles away. The challenge becomes figuring out how to maintain those family relationships. More and more people are using videoconferencing programs like Skype or social media websites for regular conversations, and some families plan to visit a couple of times a year or maybe arrange a reunion for the whole family at a site that is convenient for all. In other words, accept the limitations, but don't give up.

Contributing to society by volunteering and/or creating legacies, ranging from a personal memoir to financial resources, can also increase a sense of well-being in our later years. What do you want to leave for your children, for the community, or even for the world? These types of questions crop up, and seeking and discovering answers to them can contribute to our personal contentment. According to a Merrill Lynch report, volunteering after age 65 increases and provides an opportunity to give back.[5] The increase in memoir writing is an indication of one kind of legacy. The proliferation of community and family foundations is another. For those who can afford it, creating a family fund to support a cause you care about is yet another kind of legacy.

Well-Being at the End of Life

At the same time that we are thinking about how to adjust our attitudes and expectations for a happy life, in many cases we are facing the death or incapacity of our friends and families. Their illnesses and impending death are major transitions that can change our *roles*, *relationships*, *routines*, and *assumptions* about our place in the world. They begin to erode our anchors. We also begin to think about our own death.

Atul Gawande's book, *Being Mortal: Medicine and What Matters in the End*, brought what has been a largely taboo topic, death and dying, into the public discourse. He pointed out that medical science has improved to the point where it is possible to maintain someone's life even when the results—an extremely compromised quality of life—may actually be disastrous for the patient. Gawande strongly suggested that the job of medicine is to ensure "health and survival . . . (and) really it is larger than that. It is to enable well-being."[6]

In some cases, well-being means palliative care. Organizations like Compassion & Choices, a national nonprofit, can help you work through issues of the death and dying of people you know. Their activities include educating the public about the risks and rewards of various care choices, and advocacy to put in place national and state policies that "help patients and their loved ones advocate for care that is consistent with their values and priorities."

As we change our sense of well-being, we have a choice: We can see these changes as totally negative or we can twist the kaleidoscope and see new possibilities.

CREATE THE NEW YOU

Barbara Peters Smith, who covers aging issues for the Sarasota *Herald-Tribune*, interviewed 68-year-old John Overton about his future after he retired as CEO of the Pines, a nonprofit nursing, assisted-living, and rehabilitation center. Overton said, "To me, what is fundamental to the art of aging is simply having something to hope for, whatever that might be."[7] In other words, you need a life with a future focus, a life with meaning, a life with purpose, or as a friend said to me, "I am repurposing."

Joel's mother asked him to help his elderly father who had lost interest in his work and was becoming withdrawn. What she was asking her son to do sounded simple, but in fact it was complicated. She wanted Joel to help his father find meaning in his life. At the same time, this made Joel think about how he could avoid being in the same situation as his father is when he reaches his father's age.

What Joel's father needed was what we all need as we incorporate positive aging into our coping repertoire, which includes the following:

- Resolve your love–hate relationship with aging.
- Say no to ageism.
- Embrace change.
- Diversify your coping skills.
- Create your retirement fantasy.
- Choose your place.
- Cope with health challenges.
- Understand your family transitions.
- Keep your dance card full.
- Go for romance and/or intimacy (if you want it).
- Create your own path to positive aging.

Each of the strategies is discussed in detail throughout this book, except for the last—create your own path to positive aging. Each person's path is unique, and each person is an innovator, figuring out a way to live that is creative and building on his or her assets. The three parts that go into creating your own path are: finding your purpose, maintaining a positive attitude, and designing a life where you matter.

Finding Your Purpose: Improvise Along the Way

One of the losses we may experience as we age is a sense of our purpose in life. When you no longer have a job, and when your children are grown up and gone, you may suddenly wonder if you have a purpose or if you are just marking time. Joining your neighbors for coffee, playing bridge or golfing a couple of times a week, or just doing the housework might not seem like enough. So how can you find a purpose?

One way is to ask yourself about any regrets. What do you wish you had done earlier in life? Is it too late? Is there a piece of the dream you can capture?

Vicky is an example of capturing a dream she thought she had lost. She is someone who reinvented and repurposed herself. She had been a serial entrepreneur, moving in and out of education. When she decided to retire and stop working in a regular job at age 66, she felt it was time to revisit past passions and design a new purpose for herself. Vicky had been an English major in college and loved writing. Intrigued with the meaning of success and a successful life, she decided to write a blog filled with interviews of people expressing their views on success. This combines her identification as a boomer, her enjoyment and talent in writing, and her drive to make a difference.

In some cases, repurposing may occur as a result of a personal tragedy. Diane Rehm is a retired NPR talk show host whose husband, John, had Parkinson's disease. Because he was unable to benefit from medically assisted suicide, John starved himself to death. In her new book, *On My Own*, Rehm discussed the importance of supporting organizations like Compassion and Choices that would make it legal to help people like John instead of leaving them to consider forced starvation as an option for death.[8] Although retired from NPR, Rehm has new purpose in life—to continue her fight to make assisted suicide legal.

Another example of repurposing emerging from tragedy can be seen in Victor Strecher's work. Strecher lost his daughter when she was 19, and then he lost himself. His novel tells the story through cartoon figures of how he rediscovered himself and began to live a life of purpose.[9] We can see the necessity of having a purpose, something outside of yourself.

Now you might be asking: How can I find my purpose now that my main purpose is over? There is no surefire way to do that. Some are lucky and bump into it; others struggle to identify a new way. Mary Catherine Bateson studied women as they forged new lives. She wrote: "Each . . . has worked by improvisation, discovering the shape of our creation along the way, rather than pursuing a vision already defined . . . about the ways we combine familiar and unfamiliar components in response to new situations."[10]

To improvise implies spontaneity, ad-libbing, going with the flow, experimenting. How does someone who feels too young to be old maneuver in this new world where extra decades of life are becoming the norm? One step you can take is to revisit the possible paths outlined in Chapter 5 on retirement fantasies. This will give you an idea of the general direction you may like to take.

Maintaining a Positive Attitude—It Can Determine Your Health

Your general attitude toward life offers a clue as to how you will approach aging. The challenge is to maintain your sense of self when there are many indicators forcing a different definition. Think about your own perspective. Is your attitude positive, negative, or benign? Do you agree with those who offer a pessimistic view of getting old? Or do you have an upbeat, curious attitude toward the future?

The importance of attitude cannot be overestimated. Dr. Andrew Steptoe, an epidemiologist, psychologist, and professor at University College in London, was the lead researcher in a major longitudinal study about aging conducted in England. The data were clear: Social isolation and mortality go hand-in-hand.[11] This suggests that those with a well-defined sense of well-being, with a belief that they can control how things will go for them, and with a sense of purpose and appreciation for the good in their lives, will live longer and healthier lives.

Designing Your Life so You Feel You Matter

Morris Rosenberg, a sociologist at the University of Maryland, coined the phrase *mattering* to describe the need we all have to believe "that we count in others' lives, loom large in their thoughts, and make a difference to them."[12] When you feel that you matter, you feel sought after, appreciated, and depended on. Rosenberg identified mattering as an overlooked motive—one that explains performance, behavior, and even well-being. Mattering to oneself, to others, and to the world is the coordinating, although not the only, issue that guides our understanding of ourselves.

Rosenberg argued that mattering is a universal, lifelong need that connects us all. The concept of mattering encompasses several components: feeling that people pay attention to you, feeling that you are important, feeling that you are appreciated and depended on by others, and feeling that others take pride in you and how you handle your life. We may experience these affirmations—or lack of them—in many different ways. A retired professor, attending a conference in his field, feels marginal because he no longer is tied to his university. Conversely, a volunteer for Meals on Wheels feels appreciated for her work, and feels that people depend on her for something that is important to them.

Rosenberg studied the effects of not mattering on homeless adolescent boys in the Washington, DC, area and his wife studied the same effects on widows. With graduate students, I applied his work to adult learners and retirees. We found that institutions of higher education with practices, programs, and policies that were consciously responsive to the needs of adults had a higher percentage of adults completing their programs and were therefore happy. Rosenberg suggested that retirees who feel appreciated report feeling happy.

Many older people and many retirees complain of feeling marginalized, of not being noticed, or of not being a player. They feel out of the loop. You can have money and jewels, but if you feel sidelined or out of the loop, you will be unhappy. However, if your voice is heard, you will feel happy. To work toward ensuring your own happiness, consider the following, "A Mattering Recipe—A Way for You to Feel Appreciated." First, try to determine where you are on the mattering scale by answering a few questions:

- Do I know who I am?
- Do I appreciate myself?
- Do I feel competent?
- Are my inside and outside worlds congruent?
- Do others appreciate me?
- Do my work and community worlds make me feel needed?

On the basis of your answers, consider implementing some of the following strategies for increasing your sense that you matter, to yourself and to others.

YOUR PATH TO POSITIVE AGING

The poet Robert Browning wrote, "Grow old along with me! The best is yet to be."[13] I would suggest adding the word "maybe." Maybe the future will be wonderful, if we can figure out how to live well.

George Vaillant, study director of the Harvard Study of Adult Development, examined the data and concluded that adults can continue to grow and change in their 70s, 80s, and 90s. Specifically, Vaillant found that mature defense mechanisms like humor and patience increase, and immature defense mechanisms like projection and hypochondriasis decrease.

Vaillant also found that happiness increases with age. For example, only 18% of the study sample reported their marriage as happy, but by age 75, 76% reported their marriage as happy. Vaillant concurred with the work of Laura Carstensen, director of the Stanford Center on Longevity, who explained that as people age they tend to remember the good over the bad. Other studies confirm the relationship between age and happiness. The data are clear: There is a U-bend of happiness. People's happiness increases until their 30s, then drops in their 40s and 50s, and curves up again in their 60s and beyond. Vaillant concluded that "positive aging means to love, to work, to learn something we did not know yesterday. . . . Successful aging means giving to others . . . receiving from others, and using elegant unconscious coping mechanisms that make lemonade out of lemons."[14]

Finally, Vaillant's most important conclusion was that the major factor that promotes flourishing in old age is love. He found that love can come in adulthood and modify the traumas of early life. The opening pages of his book, *Triumphs of Experience*, start with the story of a man he called Godfrey, who came from a dysfunctional family. After medical school, Godfrey made a failed suicide attempt, but then, to everyone's surprise, developed into a mature and loving man. When Godfrey was 29, the study staff predicted he would not develop into a fully functioning professional, husband, lover, or father. His development happened gradually and resulted from the good fortune of having a loving wife and children.[14] No one factor explains the cases when adults flourish, but the main finding from the study of adult development is that when love happens, it can in fact lead to change.

If you look on the Internet for advice on how to live well, you'll find lots of recipes—eat properly, exercise, meditate, balance competing demands, attend to your spiritual life. What these varied responses suggest is that there is no one formula for all. Dr. Kevin O'Neil, the optimum life medical director for Brookdale Senior Living, is coauthor of *Optimal Aging: Your Guide From Experts in Medicine, Law, and Finance*, in which the authors point out that we need to take account of all aspects of wellness—medical, legal, psychological, physiological, and spiritual. We need to be flexible, to engage in periodic assessments of ourselves and our environment, figure out what is working, and try to discard what is not. Just as we meet with our financial advisers yearly, and often have an annual physical, we need to conduct our own "living longer, living well checkup."[15] On the basis of Vaillant's and O'Neil's work, this checkup can include tracking the answers to the following questions:

- Am I learning something new?
- Am I giving to others?
- Am I able to accept from others?
- Can I make lemonade out of lemons?
- Am I able to work, love, and play?
- Do I still have a passion that gets me going in the morning?

Revisit these questions periodically. If your answer is yes to all of them, then you clearly are living well. If you have answered no to several questions, think about some ways to make needed changes. That way you can eliminate the "maybe!"

CONCLUSION

The initial title for this chapter was "Your Road Map to Positive Aging." After interviewing a wide variety of people it became clear that there is no one road map. There may be checkpoints and there may be clues, but no single map is for everyone. Actually, improvising is a better description of how to handle finding your way in uncharted territory. First we try one thing, then we turn the kaleidoscope lens a bit more, we see life in a new way, and try something new yet again.

As we go through life's phases and transitions, one of the most effective ways to survive and maintain a positive attitude is to look to models. My friend Jeanne Hansell has been an inspiration to me. We met when we were in our early 60s. My father and her mother decided we should meet. Being obedient daughters, we followed their advice, and I have always been thankful that we did.

When I met her, Jeanne was a therapist and was starting to explore possibilities for her retirement. She found rich opportunities where others might ignore signals. After retiring, she conducted oral histories of Holocaust survivors; collected beautiful folk art; immersed herself in cultural experiences, such as music and dance in Western Massachusetts every summer; spent time at the Kripalu Center for Yoga & Health, where she learned about labyrinths and yoga; and graciously entertained those of us who arrived at her doorstep.

The surprising new path that evolved was her spiritual journey. She told me about a book that influenced her, *There Are No Accidents: Synchronicity and the Stories of Our Lives*. The author, a Jungian psychotherapist named Robert Hopcke, described chance encounters that changed lives.[16] Jeanne's chance encounter was a memorial service at a Unitarian Universalist Church. The service touched her in transformative ways, setting her on a path of extensive involvement with her newfound community. She responded to the needs in her neighborhood and began working to provide resources that would enable residents to remain in their own homes. Her later years reflected what for many may seem to be incompatible: a combination of personal decline because of health issues coupled with new growth, expansion, and vistas.

But mostly, to me, Jeanne was a wonderful friend. With all the good Jeanne did for many others, she also found time to introduce me to new experiences, to be attentive to the facts of my own life, and to my own interpretation of those facts. She made me feel good and that I mattered.

Several years ago, Jeanne self-published a book of poetry. One of her poems, "Comfort in Declining Years,"[17] foretold her openness to new experiences:

> When facing the declining years
> One looks for the eternal
> In the rushing brook.
> Its effervescent energy
> And predictable, soothing flow
> In various directions
> Suggesting new paths to follow.

The poem perfectly sums up the inspiration Jeanne continues to offer to me personally and to all who are searching for the path that—despite the detours that may occur along the way—will prove to us that the "extra years" we are being given are in fact a blessing and a source of happiness. Look around and find your inspiration.

Notes

INTRODUCTION

1. Simring, K. S. (2013). Age brings happiness. *Scientific American Mind, 24*(2).
2. Vaillant, G. E. (2002). *Aging well: Surprising guideposts to a happier life from the landmark Harvard study of adult development.* New York, NY: Little, Brown and Company. See pp. 212–213.
3. Levy, B. R., Slade, M. D., Murphy, T. E., & Gill, T. M. (2012). Association between positive age stereotypes and recovery from disability in older persons. *JAMA, 308,* 1972–1973. http://dx.doi.org/10.1001/jama.2012.14541
4. Lyubomirsky, S. (2008). *The how of happiness: A scientific approach to getting the life you want.* New York, NY: Penguin.
5. Harvard Medical School (2013). Living to 100: What's the secret? In L. S. R. Vas (Ed.), *Brain power* (pp. 228–232). Hyderabad, India: V & S.
6. Siegel, R. D., & Allison, S. M. (Eds.). (2013). *Positive psychology: Harnessing the power of happiness, mindfulness, and inner strength.* Cambridge, MA: Harvard Medical Publications, p. 8.
7. Friedan, B. (1993). *The fountain of age.* New York, NY: Simon & Schuster.

CHAPTER 1: TALK BACK TO YOUR MIRROR

1. Adelson, A. (2015, February 24). Last word: The French do it better. *Barnard Magazine*, p. 76.
2. American Society of Plastic Surgeons. (2013). *2013 plastic surgery statistics: Statistical report of the cosmetic surgery age distribution (55 and over)* (p. 18). Retrieved from American Society of Plastic Surgeons website: https://d2wirczt3b6wjm.cloudfront.net/News/Statistics/2013/plastic-surgery-statistics-full-report-2013.pdf
3. BCC Research. (2016). *Antiaging products and services: The global market.* (Report HLC060C). Retrieved from http://www.bccresearch.com/market-research/healthcare/anti-aging-products-services-report-hlc060C.html
4. Colby, S. L., & Ortman, J. M. (2015). *Projections of the size and composition of the U.S. Population: 2014 to 2060* (U.S. Census Bureau Report P25-1143). Retrieved from http://www.census.gov/content/dam/Census/library/publications/2015/demo/p25-1143.pdf
5. Fishman, T. C. (2010). *Shock of gray: The aging population of the world's population and how it pits young against old, child against parent, worker against boss, company against rival, and nation against nation.* New York, NY: Scribner.
6. Taylor, P., Morin, R., Parker, K., Cohn, D., & Wang, W. (2009). *Growing old in America: Expectations vs. reality.* Retrieved from Pew Research Center website: http://www.pewsocialtrends.org/2009/06/29/growing-old-in-america-expectations-vs-reality/
7. Howard, B. (2012). What to expect in your 70s and beyond: The good and bad. Plus advice on feeling happy, sexy and pain-free. *AARP the Magazine.* Retrieved from http://www.aarp.org/health/healthy-living/info-09-2012/what-to-expect-in-your-70s-and-beyond.html

CHAPTER 2: JUST SAY NO TO AGEISM

1. Wilkinson, J. A., & Ferraro, K. F. (2002). Thirty years of ageism research. In T. D. Nelson (Ed.), *Ageism: Stereotyping and prejudice against older persons* (pp. 339–358). Cambridge, MA: MIT Press.
2. Gerbner, G., & Signorielli, N. (1979). *Women and minorities in television drama, 1969–1978*. Philadelphia: University of Pennsylvania.
3. Perry Graham, N. (2010). Aging's not optional. *AARP the Magazine.* Retrieved from http://www.aarp.org/personal-growth/life-stories/info-11-2009/estreet_JF10_aging_optional.html
4. Rampellfeb, C. (2013, February 3). In hard economy for all ages, older isn't better . . . it's brutal. *New York Times*, p. A1.
5. Black, K., & Gregory, S. (2011). *Aging with dignity and independence initiative: Actionable themes: Issues and opportunities.* Sarasota: University of South Florida.
6. Markus, H., & Nurius, P. (1986). Possible selves. *American Psychologist, 41,* 954–969. http://dx.doi.org/10.1037/0003-066X.41.9.954
7. Jenkins, J. A. (2016). *Disrupt aging: A bold new path to living your best life at every age.* New York, NY: PublicAffairs.
8. Harvard School of Public Health & Metropolitan Life Foundation. (2004). *Reinventing aging: Baby boomers and civic engagement.* Retrieved from the AARP website: http://assets.aarp.org/rgcenter/general/boomers_engagement.pdf
9. Castle, S. (Executive Producer), & WNYC Radio (Creator). (2009). *In the mix: Bridging the years . . . teens & seniors mix it up* [Television series]. Retrieved from http://www.pbs.org/inthemix/shows/show_bridingtheyears.html

10. Bahrampour, T. (2016, January 23). We're lucky if we get to be old, physician and professor believes. *The Washington Post*. Retrieved from https://www.washingtonpost.com/local/social-issues/were-lucky-if-we-get-to-be-old-physician-and-professor-believes/2016/01/23/251ed8b2-b9c2-11e5-829c-26ffb874a18d_story.html

11. Palmore, E. (1980). The facts on aging quiz: A review of findings. *The Gerontologist, 20*, 669–672.

CHAPTER 3: EMBRACE CHANGE

1. Bernstein, E. (2009, July 28). Moving time, and the feeling is queasy. *The Wall Street Journal*. Retrieved from http://www.wsj.com/articles/SB10001424052970204900904574306232392067404

2. Hagestad, G. O. (1996). On-time, off-time, out of time? Reflections on continuity and discontinuity from an illness process. In V. L. Bengston (Ed.), *Adulthood and aging: Research on continuities and discontinuities* (pp. 204–222). New York, NY: Springer.

3. Neugarten, B. L., Moore, J. W., & Lowe, J. C. (1965). Age norms, age constraints, and adult socialization. *American Journal of Sociology, 70*, 710–717.

4. Lawrence-Lightfoot, S. (2012). *Exit: The endings that set us free*. New York, NY: Sara Crichton Books, p. 9.

CHAPTER 4: DIVERSIFY YOUR COPING SKILLS

1. Angell, R. (2014, February 17). This old man: Life in the nineties. *The New Yorker*, p. 63.

2. Lazarus, R. S., & Folkman, S. (1984). *Stress, appraisal, and coping*. New York, NY: Springer. See p. 24.

3. Pearlin, L. I., & Schooler, C. (1978). The structure of coping. *Journal of Health and Social Behavior, 19*, 2–21.

4. Gilbert, D. (2005). *Stumbling on happiness*. New York, NY: Random House.

5. Moen, P., Sweet, S., & Hill, R. (2010). Risk, resilience, and life-course fit: Older couples' encores following job loss. In P. S. Fry & C. L. M. Keyes (Eds.), *New frontiers in resilient aging: Life-strengths and well-being in late life* (pp. 283–309). New York, NY: Cambridge University Press.

6. Bombeck, E. (1991, July 30). Flattery will get you anywhere. *Ocala Star-Banner*, p. 8A.

7. Hyatt, C., & Gottlieb, L. (1987). *When smart people fail*. New York, NY: Simon & Schuster.

8. Brown, S. (2009). *Play: How it shapes the brain, opens the imagination, and invigorates the soul*. New York, NY: Penguin.

9. Ameli, R. (2014). *25 lessons in mindfulness: Now time for healthy living*. Washington, DC: American Psychological Association.

10. Commito, L. (2011). *Love is the new currency: Creating a new measure of wealth*. New Delhi, India: CorEssence.

11. Kay, S., & Schlossberg, N. K. (2014). *Transition guide: A new way to think about change*. Salt Lake City, UT: TransitionWorks, Inc.

CHAPTER 5: CREATE YOUR OWN RETIREMENT FANTASY

1. Schlossberg, N. (2009). *Revitalizing retirement: Reshaping your identity, relationships, and purpose*. Washington, DC: American Psychological Association.

2. Moen, P., & Fields, V. (2002). Midcourse in the United States: Does unpaid community participation replace paid work? *Ageing International, 27*(3), 21–48.

3. Eisner, D., Grimm, R. T., Maynard, S., & Washburn, S. (2009). The new volunteer workforce. *Stanford Social*

Innovation Review, 7(1), 1–11. Retrieved from http://ssir. org/articles/entry/the_new_volunteer_workforce

4. Freedman, M. (2007). *Encore: Finding work that matters in the second half of life.* New York, NY: PublicAffairs.

5. Sightings, T. (2015, July 20). 10 worries older Americans face. *U.S. News and World Report.* Retrieved from http://money.usnews.com/money/blogs/on-retirement/ 2015/07/20/10-worries-older-americans-face

6. DeNavas-Walt, C., & Proctor, B. D. (2015). *Income & poverty in the United States: Current population reports* (Report No. P60-252). Washington, DC: U.S. Department of Commerce. Retrieved from http://www.census.gov/ content/dam/Census/library/publications/2015/demo/ p60-252.pdf

7. Krumboltz, J., & Levin, A. (2004). *Luck is no accident: Making the most of happenstance in your life and career.* Atascadero, CA: Impact.

CHAPTER 6: CHOOSE YOUR PLACE: LOCATION, LOCATION, LOCATION

1. Gladwell, M. (2008). *Outliers: The story of success.* New York, NY: Little, Brown and Company, p. 7.

2. Fishman, T. C. (2010). *Shock of gray: The aging of the world's population and how it pits young against old, child against parent, worker against boss, company against rival, and nation against nation.* New York, NY: Scribner, p. 231.

3. Lowrey, A. (2014, March 15). Income gap, meet the longevity gap. *The New York Times.* Retrieved from http://www.nytimes.com/2014/03/16/business/income- gap-meet-the-longevity-gap.html?_r=0, para. 1.

4. Baker, B. (2014). *With a little help from our friends: Creating community as we grow older.* Nashville, TN: Vanderbilt University Press, p. 3.

5. Ornstein, K. A., Leff, B., Covinsky, K. E., Ritchie, C. S., Federman, A. D., Roberts, L., . . . Szanton, S. L. (2015). Epidemiology of the homebound population in the United States. *JAMA Internal Medicine, 175*, p. 1180. http://dx.doi.org/10.1001/jamainternmed.2015.1849

6. AARP. (n.d.). *Caring for a difficult older adult.* Retrieved from http://www.aarp.org/relationships/caregiving-resource-center/info-09-2010/pc_caring_for_a_difficult_older_adult.html

7. Barrett, W. P. (2015, February 11). The best foreign retirement havens for 2015. *Forbes.* Retrieved from http://www.forbes.com/sites/williampbarrett/2015/02/11/the-best-foreign-retirement-havens-for-2015/#547dd263bb16

8. Rodin, J., & Timko, C. (1992). Sense of control, aging, and health. In M. G. Ory, R. P. Abeles, & D. D. Lipman (Eds.), *Aging health and behavior* (pp. 174–206). Newbury Park, CA: Sage.

9. American Psychiatric Association. (2013). *Diagnostic and statistical manual of mental disorders* (5th ed.). Arlington, VA: Author.

10. Luhrmann, T. M. (2015, May 25). How places let us feel the past. *The New York Times.* Retrieved from http://www.nytimes.com/2015/05/25/opinion/how-places-let-us-feel-the-past.html

11. World Health Organization. (2016). *Towards an age-friendly world.* Retrieved from http://www.who.int/ageing/age-friendly-world/en/

CHAPTER 7: COPE WITH HEALTH CHALLENGES

1. Lazarus, R., & Folkman, S. (1984). *Stress, appraisal and coping.* New York, NY: Springer.

2. Running Wolf, P., & Rickard, J. A. (2003). Talking circles: A Native American approach to experiential learn-

ing. *Journal of Multicultural Counseling and Development, 31*(1), 39–43.

3. Alzheimer's Association. (2016). *About frontotemporal dementia*. Retrieved from http://www.alz.org/dementia/fronto-temporal-dementia-ftd-symptoms.asp

4. Boehm, J., Vie, L., & Kubzansky, L. (2012). The promise of well-being interventions for improving health risk behaviors. *Current Cardiovascular Risk Reports, 6,* 511–519. http://dx.doi.org/10.1007/s12170-012-0273-x

5. Harvard School of Public Health. (2011). *The biology of emotion—And what it may teach us about helping people to live longer*. Retrieved from https://www.hsph.harvard.edu/news/magazine/happiness-stress-heart-disease/

6. Langer, E. J. (2009). *Counter clockwise: Mindful health and the power of possibility*. New York, NY: Ballantine Books, p. 184.

7. Mindfulness. (n.d.). In *Merriam-Webster's online dictionary* (11th ed.). Retrieved from http://www.merriam-webster.com/dictionary/mindfulness

8. Langer, E. J., & Rodin, J. (1976). The effects of choice and enhanced personal responsibility for the aged: A field experiment in an institutional setting. *Journal of Personality and Social Psychology, 34,* 191–198.

9. Lachman, M. E. (2005). Aging under control? *Psychological Science Agenda, 19*(1).

10. Banerjee, S. (2015). *Utilization patterns and out-of-pocket expenses for different health care services among American retirees* (Research Report 411). Employee Benefit Research Institute, Washington, DC.

11. Castleman, M. (2012, December 12). Great sex without intercourse: Older couples can look forward to trying out these creative alternatives. *AARP*. Retrieved from http://www.aarp.org/home-family/sex-intimacy/info-12-2012/great-sex-without-intercourse.html

CHAPTER 8: UNDERSTAND YOUR FAMILY TRANSITIONS

1. Roberts, S. (2013, September 20). Divorce after 50 grows more common. *The New York Times.* Retrieved from http://www.nytimes.com/2013/09/22/fashion/weddings/divorce-after-50-grows-more-common.html

2. Skolnick, A. S., & Skolnick, J. H. (Eds.). (2007). *Family in transition* (14th ed.). Boston, MA: Allyn & Bacon.

3. Fry, R., Passel, J., & Pew Research Center. (2014). *In post-recession era, young adults drive continuing rise in multi-generational living.* Retrieved from Pew Research Center website: http://www.pewsocialtrends.org/2014/07/17/in-post-recession-era-young-adults-drive-continuing-rise-in-multi-generational-living/

4. Hagestad, G. O. (1981). Problems and promises in the social psychology of intergenerational relations. In R. W. Fogel & J. G. March (Eds.), *Aging: Stability and change in the family* (pp. 11–46). New York, NY: Academic Press.

5. Haruf, K. (2015). *Our souls at night.* New York, NY: Alfred A. Knopf.

6. Goyer, A. (2010, December 20). More grandparents raising grandkids: New census data shows an increase in children being raised by extended family. Retrieved from AARP website: http://www.aarp.org/relationships/grandparenting/info-12-2010/more_grandparents_raising_grandchildren.html

7. Pinson-Millburn, N. M., Fabian, E., Schlossberg, N. K., & Pyle, M. (1996). Grandparents raising grandchildren. *Journal of Counseling & Development, 74,* 548–554.

8. Pirnot, K. H. (2015). *Nothing left to burn.* Seattle, WA: Create Space Independent Publishing.

9. National Alliance for Caregiving, & AARP Public Policy Institute. (2015). *Caregiving in the U.S.* Washington, DC:

AARP Public Policy Institute. Retrieved from http://
www.caregiving.org/wp-content/uploads/2015/05/2015_
CaregivingintheUS_Final-Report-June-4_WEB.pdf

10. SAGE & Movement Advancement Project. (2010). *Improving the lives of LGBT older adults.* Retrieved from http://www.lgbtmap.org/file/improving-the-lives-of-lgbt-older-adults.pdf

11. Sheehy, G. (Ed.). (2010). *Passages in caregiving: Turning chaos into confidence.* New York, NY: Harper Collins.

12. Hagestad, G. O. (1996). On-time, off-time, out of time? Reflections on continuity and discontinuity from an illness process. In V. L. Bengston (Ed.), *Adulthood and aging: Research on continuities and discontinuities.* New York, NY: Springer.

13. Lawrence-Lightfoot, S. (2012). *Exit: The endings that set us free.* New York, NY: Sara Crichton Books.

14. Arnold, A. P., & Zonder, L. R. (2016). *Collaborative divorce: A win-win approach.* Retrieved from http://www.vcba.org/2016/08/collaborative-divorce-a-win-win-approach-by-alice-p-arnold-lisa-r-zonder/

15. Enright, R. D. (2001). *Forgiveness is a choice: A step-by-step process for resolving anger and restoring hope.* Washington, DC: American Psychological Association.

CHAPTER 9: KEEP YOUR DANCE CARD FULL: PAY ATTENTION TO FRIENDS, FAMILY, AND FUN

1. Vaillant, G. (2012). *Triumphs of experience: The men of the Harvard grant study.* Cambridge, MA: Harvard University Press, p. 27.

2. Waldinger, R. (2015, November). *What makes a good life? Lessons from the longest study on happiness.* Talk presented at TEDxBeaconStreet, Brookline, MA.

3. Weiss, R. (1973). *Loneliness: The experience of emotional and social isolation.* Cambridge, MA: MIT Press.

4. Edmondson, B. (2010). All the lonely people. *AARP the Magazine*. Retrieved from http://www.aarp.org/personal-growth/transitions/info-09-2010/all_the_lonely_people.html

5. Bowlby, J. (1980). *Loss: Sadness and depression*. New York, NY: Basic Books

6. Bartholomew, K., & Duck, S. (Eds.). (1993). *Learning about relationships. Understanding relationship processes series* (Vol. 2, pp. 30–62). Thousand Oaks, CA: Sage.

7. Kahn, R. L., & Antonucci, T. E. (1980). Convoys over the life course: Attachment, roles, and social support. In P. B. Baltes & O. G. Brim (Eds.), *Life-span development and behavior* (pp. 383–405). New York, NY: Academic Press.

8. Rubin, L. (1985). *Just friends*. New York, NY: Harper Collins, p. 11.

9. Berkowitz, G. (2002). UCLA study on friendship among women. *Professional Women's Network*. Retrieved from https://scholar.google.com/scholar?q=ucla+study+on+friendship+among+women&btnG=&hl=en&as_sdt=0%2C10

10. Taylor, T. (2015, November 9). *Older adults on social media*. Retrieved from https://www.theseniorlist.com/2015/11/older-adults-on-social-media/

11. Madden, M. (2010, August 27). *Older adults and social media*. Retrieved from http://www.pewinternet.org/2010/08/27/older-adults-and-social-media/

12. Smith, A. (2014, April 3). *Older adults and technology use*. Retrieved from http://www.pewinternet.org/2014/04/03/older-adults-and-technology-use/

13. Cohen, G. (2005). *The mature mind: The positive power of the aging brain*. New York, NY: Basic Books.

14. From *Rewards of dancing as you age: Dancing regularly can help revitalize your mind and your body*, by E. Hoffman, 2015. Retrieved from http://www.nextavenue.org/

rewards-of-dancing-as-you-age/. Copyright 2015 by Twin Cities Public Television. Reprinted with permission.

15. Hoffman, E. (2015, June 29). *Rewards of dancing as you age: Dancing regularly can help revitalize your mind and your body.* Retrieved from http://www.nextavenue.org/ rewards-of-dancing-as-you-age/

16. Gladwell, M. (2002). *The tipping point: How little things can make a difference.* New York, NY: Little, Brown and Company.

CHAPTER 10: GO FOR ROMANCE
(IF YOU WANT IT)

1. Economics and Statistics Administration, U.S. Department of Commerce. (1995). *Sixty-five plus in the United States* (U.S. Census Bureau Statistical Brief). Retrieved from http://www.census.gov/population/socdemo/stat briefs/agebrief.html

2. Todd, D. (2012, May 29). Never too old. *Pittsburgh Post-Gazette*, p. A7.

3. Montenegro, X. P. (2003, September). Lifestyles, dating, and romance: A study of midlife singles. *AARP the Magazine.* Retrieved from http://assets.aarp.org/rgcenter/ general/singles_1.pdf

4. Castleman, M. (2012, December 12). Great sex without intercourse: Older couples can look forward to trying out these creative alternatives. Retrieved from AARP website: http://www.aarp.org/home-family/sex-intimacy/ info-12-2012/great-sex-without-intercourse.html

5. Livingston, G. (2014). *Four-in-ten couples are saying "I do" again: Growing numbers of adults have remarried.* Retrieved from Pew Research Center website: http://www. pewsocialtrends.org/2014/11/14/four-in-ten-couples-are-saying-i-do-again/

6. Match Up To Date. (2011, November 16). *Molly and Ed: Love is still in the air at 90 & 82*. Retrieved from http://blog.match.com/2011/11/16/molly-and-ed-love-is-still-in-the-air-at-90-and-82/

7. Sills, J. (2009). *Getting naked again*. New York, NY: Springboard Press.

CHAPTER 11. CREATE YOUR OWN HAPPINESS: YOUR PATH TO POSITIVE AGING

1. Moody, H. R. (2016, March 5). *Human values in aging: Disillusionment* (Electronic Mailing List). Washington, DC: AARP.

2. Josselson, R. (1987). *Finding herself: Pathways to identity development in women*. San Francisco, CA: Jossey Bass, p. 10.

3. Angell, R. (2014, February 24). This old man: Life in the nineties. *The New Yorker*, p. 63.

4. Brim, O. G. (1992). *Ambition: How we manage success and failure throughout our lives*. New York, NY: HarperCollins.

5. Merrill Lynch. (2015). *Giving in retirement: America's longevity bonus*. Charlotte, NC: Bank of America Corporation. Retrieved from https://mlaem.fs.ml.com/content/dam/ML/Articles/pdf/ML_AgeWave_Giving_in_Retirement_Report.pdf

6. Gawande, A. (2014). *Being mortal: Medicine and what matters in the end*. New York, NY: Metropolitan Books, p. 252.

7. Peters Smith, B. (2012, April 12). What makes older people happy? *Herald-Tribune*. Retrieved from http://health.heraldtribune.com/2013/04/12/what-makes-older-people-happy/

8. Rehm, D. (2016). *On my own*. New York, NY: Alfred A. Knopf.

9. Strecher, V. J. (2013). *On purpose: Lessons in life and health from the frog, the dung beetle, and Julia.* Ann Arbor, MI: Dung Beetle Press.

10. Bateson, M. C. (1989). *Composing a life.* New York, NY: Grove Press, p. 1.

11. Steptoe, A., Shankar, A., Demakakos, P., & Wardle, J. (2013). Social isolation, loneliness, and all-cause mortality in older men and women. *Proceedings of the National Academies of Sciences of the United States of America, 110,* 5797–5801. http://dx.doi.org/10.1073/pnas.1219686110

12. Rosenberg, M., & McCullough, B. C. (1981). Mattering: Inferred significance to parents and mental health among adolescents. *Research in Community and Mental Health, 2,* p. 163.

13. Browning, R. (n.d.). *Rabbi Ben Ezra.* Retrieved from http://www.poetryfoundation.org/poems-and-poets/poems/detail/43775

14. Vaillant, G. (2012). *Triumphs of experience: The men of the Harvard grant study.* Cambridge, MA: Harvard University Press, p. 61.

15. O'Neil, K., & Peterson, R. L. (2004). *Optimal aging: Your guide from experts in medicine, law and finance.* Sarasota, FL: Optimal Aging LLC.

16. Hopcke, R. H. (1997). *There are no accidents: Synchronicity and the stories of our lives.* New York, NY: Riverhead Books.

17. From *The Tension of Opposites: A Memoir in Poetry* (p. 100), by J. H. Hansell, 2007, Washington, DC: Author. Copyright 2007 by Jeanne Harris Hansell. Reprinted with permission.

Index

About the Author

Nancy K. Schlossberg, EdD, is Professor Emerita, Department of Counseling and Personnel Services, College of Education at the University of Maryland. She previously served on the faculties of Wayne State University, Howard University, and Pratt Institute. She was the first woman executive at the American Council of Education (ACE), where she established the Office of Women in Higher Education (1973). She later served as a senior Fellow at ACE's Center on Adult Learning.

She has published nine books, including *Counseling Adults in Transition: Linking Schlossberg's Theory With Practice in a Diverse World* (4th ed., 2012, with M. L. Anderson and J. Goodman); *Revitalizing Retirement: Reshaping Your Identity, Relationships, and Purpose* (2009); *Overwhelmed: Coping With Life's Ups and Downs* (2nd ed., 2007, with M. Evans); *Retire Smart, Retire Happy: Finding Your True Path in Life* (2004); *Getting the Most Out of College* (2001, with A. Chickering); and *Going to Plan B* (1996, with S. Robinson).

Dr. Schlossberg has delivered more than 100 keynote addresses and has been quoted in cover stories in *USA Today*, *The New York Times*, *The Wall Street Journal*, Sarasota's *Herald-Tribune*, *Reader's Digest*, *Family Circle*, *Better Homes and Gardens*, *U.S. News & World Report*, and *Consumer Reports*. She was featured in a 90-minute PBS Pledge Special in June 2007, "Retire Smart, Retire Happy."

Dr. Schlossberg is a Fellow in three American Psychological Association (APA) divisions; Fellow, Gerontological Association; APA's G. Stanley Hall Lecturer on Adult Development; and Distinguished Scholar at the University of Maryland. She has received awards from The National Career Development Association, National Association of Student Personnel Administrators, and American College Personnel Association. She recently received the 2016 Teachers College Columbia University Distinguished Alumni Award.